D1065510

Stendhal Revisited

Twayne's World Authors Series
French Literature

David O'Connell, Editor
Georgia State University

TWAS 839

Stendhal
Photograph of Dedreux-Dorcy portrait courtesy Musée Stendhal, Grenoble

Stendhal Revisited

Emile J. Talbot

University of Illinois at Urbana-Champaign

Twayne Publishers ■ New York

Maxwell Macmillan Canada ■ Toronto

Maxwell Macmillan International ■ New York Oxford Singapore Sydney

Stendhal Revisited
Emile J. Talbot

Copyright 1993 by Twayne Publishers

Twayne Publishers
Macmillan Publishing Company
866 Third Avenue
New York, New York 10022

Maxwell Macmillan Canada, Inc.
1200 Eglinton Avenue East
Suite 200
Don Mills, Ontario M3C 3N1

Library of Congress Cataloging-in-Publication Data

Talbot, Emile
  Stendhal revisited / Emile J. Talbot.
    p. cm. – (Twayne's world authors series; TWAS 839)
  Includes bibliographical references and index.
  ISBN 0-8057-8288-5 (alk. paper)
  1. Stendhal, 1783-1842 – Criticism and interpretation. I. Title.
II. Series.
PQ2441.T35 1993
848'.709 – dc20   93-19370
                                                              CIP

The paper used in this publication meets the minimum requirements of American National Standard for Information Sciences – Permanence of Paper for Printed Library Materials, ANSI Z39.48-1984.

10 9 8 7 6 5 4 3 2 1

Printed in the United States of America.

for Elizabeth

Contents

Preface

Stendhal, long recognized as one of the giants of French literature, has over the years attracted an enormous amount of critical commentary. This brief book cannot do justice to the author nor to the commentary, much of it excellent. I have attempted to acknowledge my debt to other critics, but it is likely that over many years of reading Stendhal criticism some insights I have gathered from other commentators have become internalized to the point that I am no longer aware of their origins. To the extent that this has occurred, I here express my gratitude to those who have influenced me in this manner.

Within the space available, I have tried to reflect current thinking, including my own, on Stendhal in a way that is accessible to a general audience. I have deliberately avoided one current of Stendhal criticism, more fashionable in the past than at present, which views Stendhal's work as literary solipsism, as a reflection of Stendhal the man. Consequently, I have not dwelt on Stendhal's life, about which a great deal is known, although I give a rapid survey of it in Chapter 1, in which I also provide an overview of Stendhal's nonfiction and nonautobiographical work. The balance of this study focuses on his fiction and autobiography exclusively.

Some aspects of my discussion in Chapter 2 appeared in an earlier version in *French Forum* (1978).

Bibliographic Note

All my quotations from Stendhal are taken from the 50-volume edition of his works edited by V. Del Litto and E. Abravanel (Geneva: Cercle du Bibliophile, 1967-74). The references are cited in the text as follows:

A	*Armance*
CP	*The Charterhouse of Parma (La Chartreuse de Parme)*; 2 vols.
IC	*The Italian Chronicles (Chroniques italiennes)*; 2 vols.
J	*Journal*; 4 vols.
L	*Lamiel*
HB	*The Life of Henry Brulard (Vie de Henry Brulard)*; 2 vols.
LL	*Lucien Leuwen*; 4 vols.
ME	*Memoirs of Egotism (Mémoires d'égotisme)*
M	*Miscellany (Mélanges)*; 5 vols.
OL	*On Love (De l'Amour)*; 2 vols.
RS	*Racine and Shakespeare (Racine et Shakespeare)*
RB	*The Red and the Black (Le Rouge et le Noir)*; 2 vols.
S	*Stories (Romans et Nouvelles)*

Quotations from the correspondence are taken from the three-volume edition by H. Martineau and V. Del Litto in the Bibliothèque de la Pléïade (Paris: Gallimard, 1962-68) and cited in the text as *Corr.*

All italics within quotations are those of the author quoted. All translations from the French are my own.

Chronology

1783	Henri Beyle (Stendhal) born in Grenoble 23 January.
1790	Stendhal's mother, Henriette Beyle, dies.
1796	Stendhal begins a three-year course of study at the Central School in Grenoble.
1799	Arrives in Paris to attend the Polytechnical School but does not take the entrance examinations.
1800-1801	Becomes a clerk at the War Ministry and then is incorporated into the army as a second lieutenant. Makes first trip to Italy.
1805	Resides in Marseilles; has liaison with Mélanie Guilbert, an actress.
1806-1809	Is civilian administrator in French-occupied German lands.
1810-1814	Is commissioner of the Council of State.
1812	Participates in Napoleon's Russian campaign.
1814-1821	Resides in Italy.
1815	*Vies de Haydn, de Mozart et de Métastase* (*The Lives of Haydn, Mozart, and Metastasio*).
1817	*Histoire de la peinture en Italie* (*The History of Italian Painting*) and *Rome, Naples et Florence en 1817* (*Rome, Naples, and Florence in 1817*).
1818-1821	Period of unrequited love for Mathilde Dembowski.
1821-1830	Resides in Paris.
1822	*De l'Amour* (*On Love*).
1823	*Racine et Shakespeare* (*Racine and Shakespeare*) and *Vie de Rossini* (*The Life of Rossini*).

1824-1826	Has liaison with Clémentine Curial.
1825	*Racine and Shakespeare No. II* and *D'un nouveau complot contre les industriels* (*Concerning a New Plot against Industrialists*).
1827	New edition of *Rome, Naples, and Florence*; publication of *Armance*.
1829	*Promenades dans Rome* (*Walks in Rome*).
1830	*Le Rouge et le Noir* (*The Red and the Black*).
1831-1842	Is French consul at Civitavecchia in the Papal States.
1836-1839	On leave from his diplomatic post, resides in Paris.
1838	*Mémoires d'un touriste* (*Memoirs of a Tourist*).
1839	*La Chartreuse de Parme* (*The Charterhouse of Parma*).
1842	Dies in Paris on 23 March.

Chapter One

The Man and the Writer

Childhood and Youth

The man we have come to call Stendhal was born Marie-Henri Beyle on 23 January 1783 in Grenoble, then a town of 25,000 inhabitants. Although its roots were in the peasantry, the family had been firmly middle class for several generations. Stendhal's father was a lawyer and his maternal grandfather the town's most respected doctor. His early childhood appears to have been a happy one, until the death of his mother in childbirth when he was seven. Such an event would be difficult for any child, but it was all the more so for the hypersensitive Stendhal, whose love for his mother was out of the ordinary. In his autobiography Stendhal recounts his passion for his mother in graphic, erotic terms that have led psychoanalytically minded critics to evoke the Oedipal complex. What is certain is that the event marked him indelibly. Overhearing a priest trying to console his father by telling him that his wife's death was God's will, the boy decided then and there, he recounts more than 40 years later, that he could not accept such a God. His rebellion against God and the Church that purported to represent him extended to a revolt against paternal authority.

Stendhal's strong dislike for his father, whom he describes in the most negative terms, was real. He particularly took umbrage at his father's alliance, after his mother's death, with his Aunt Séraphie, his mother's sister, whom he describes as an embittered spinster who reveled at making his life difficult. He detested his tutor, a priest named Raillane, who treated him despotically. These three formed what he called "the clan of the tyrants" and while there is ample evidence to suggest that his description of this trio is highly exaggerated, there can be no question but that he resented them enormously. His revolt against them was largely passive, except when it came to politics, where he adopted and flaunted the republican ideals of the Revolution, much to the scandal of his royalist family.

The "clan of tyrants" did not constitute, however, the entire family entourage. Stendhal's maternal grandfather, Dr. Gagnon, a cultivated, courtly man, had an impressive library and was known locally as a progressive thinker. Stendhal very much admired him, felt comfortable with him, and sought him out frequently. As his own father became more sullen and withdrawn after his mother's death, Grandfather Gagnon became a father figure for him. If Stendhal remained throughout his life marked by the ideals of the Enlightenment, the origins of this attitude can be traced directly to Grandfather Gagnon. The young boy also felt comfortable with his Great-aunt Elizabeth, whose highly developed sense of honor he very much admired, and his Uncle Romain Gagnon, known as the Don Juan of the town, who became for his young nephew a model of the worldly-wise bon vivant. He retained fond memories of these three, even if, in later years, his memory seems to have focused on the "tyrants."

Having no childhood friends other than his sister Pauline (his family would not let him play with other children) and detesting his father, his Aunt Séraphie, and his tutors, young Henri Beyle found some pleasure at the family's country home at Claix and at his uncle's home at Les Echelles in nearby Savoy, but his satisfaction came mainly from literature. A precociously voracious reader, he seems to have taken special delight in books filched from his father's, his grandfather's, and his uncle's libraries. He thereby had access to a wide range of literature, including not only the French classics but also foreign writers such as Ariosto, Cervantes, and Shakespeare, not to mention licentious novels from his Uncle Romain's collection.

When the opening of a Central School in Grenoble was announced, Stendhal, then 13, understandably rejoiced. Since Dr. Gagnon was on the board that had planned and organized this institution, the family could not very well prevent him from attending. For three years Stendhal was a student at this school, the only formal education he would ever receive. He had expected to find fellow students who were imbued as he was with chivalric ideals of honor and manly camaraderie. Instead he found ruffians, careerists, or snobs, and it took some time before he made friends, although some of these friends were to remain so for many years. More importantly, perhaps, the Central School, which had been organized according to the ideals of the philosopher Etienne Bonnot de Condillac, was to confirm an empirical side to his thought and strengthen his interests in logical thinking. By his last year Stendhal had become a star student in mathematics, a subject to which he devoted himself with great zeal. This devotion to mathematics seems to have been motivated partly by a genuine respect for an intellectual discipline that could not be subverted by ideological concerns and partly as an avenue out of Grenoble, a city he had grown to despise. His mathematical skills and honors convinced the family to allow him to go to Paris to enter the Polytechnical School. It is while he was on his way to Paris that he learned that Napoleon had staged a coup d'état and was now in full control of the government.

The Apprenticeship of Love and Letters

Stendhal arrived in Paris on 10 November 1799 and was immediately disappointed with the city he had so long dreamed of. It seemed dirty, its people shabby, and there were no mountains to be seen. He did not present himself for the entrance examinations for the Polytechnical School, deciding instead to pursue his fantasy of becoming a great playwright. However, he soon fell quite ill and might not have recovered were it not that Noël Daru, a cousin of his grandfather's, learned about his plight, had him brought to his house and attended to by his own doctor. Stendhal was not too happy in this bourgeois household, although he became quite friendly with the younger son, Martial, a fun-loving Don Juan type not unlike Stendhal's Uncle Romain. For his part, Noël Daru was not amused at his cousin's failure to take the entrance exams at the Polytechnical nor with his evident willingness to lead what seemed to him an idle life. Consequently he announced to Stendhal one day that his son Pierre, then a rising star in Napoleon's bureaucracy, would take him to work at the War Ministry. Stendhal did not enjoy working as a clerk, but the job did provide him some income to supplement the allowance he was getting from home. Moreover, after three months, he was given the opportunity to accompany the Daru brothers to Italy in conjunction with Napoleon's campaign there. He arrived in Milan in June 1800.

Stendhal's discovery of Milan and northern Italy was for him a revelation. The sheer beauty of the area was such that he could never forget it. Italian music, which he now encountered for the first time, seemed to him heavenly. And Italian women overwhelmed him by their beauty, sensitivity, and freedom with their affections. He became infatuated with one such woman, Angela Pietragrua, to whom he did not declare himself but who would remain in his mind for more than a decade. For him, Angela was the symbol of high passion that he thought only Italian women were capable of.

Through his cousin Pierre's influence, Stendhal, then only 17, was made a second lieutenant in the dragoons and later aide-de-camp to General Michaud. His powerful connections could have led him far in the military, and there is every evidence that Pierre Daru was willing to continue to use his influence to help him. But Stendhal, soon unhappy with military life, became ill, returned to France, and resigned his commission. Since his goal was still to become a great playwright, he began to take acting lessons, which he hoped would give him a better feel for dramaturgy while ridding him of his regional accent and placing him in the proximity of young actresses. He did meet one young actress, Mélanie Guilbert, with whom he quickly fell in love. When she accepted a job in a theatrical company in Marseilles, Stendhal, who had himself been contemplating moving to Marseilles as a partner in a produce import business, decided to follow her there. His partnership, however, required a large sum of money, which he was hoping to obtain from his family. His father, this time supported by his grandfather, refused. The family's judgment that the operation was too risky would prove to be a correct one, for the British blockade would soon devastate the Marseilles import business. Stendhal went to Marseilles nevertheless (again with an allowance from the family) and took a job as a clerk in the same import firm where he had planned to be a partner.

It is here that Mélanie finally yielded to him. The numerous letters to his sister attest to his conviction that Mélanie was the most sensitive and intelligent woman on earth. Within months, however, he had tired of her and did not protest much when she had to return to Paris to pursue her acting career there. He stayed on in Marseilles another three months, knowing that he too would have to move on, since the import business was clearly floundering. Once again, he turned to his cousin, Pierre Daru, imploring him to obtain a position in the imperial administration for him. Pierre, however, was not eager to do so, considering that his young cousin had acted irresponsibly in resigning a commission he had obtained for him. Finally, Stendhal decided to return to Paris anyway and was able to persuade Martial Daru to take him to Germany with him. There, again through the influence of the Daru family, he was given important and responsible positions in the administration of France's new German territories.

Having now become a respected government official with a decent income, he attempted to win the affections of a young German woman, Wilhelmine von Griesheim. She welcomed his kindness and attention but was not interested in pursuing the relationship further. By the time he returned to Paris in 1809, however, he was already pining for his benefactor's wife, Alexandrine Daru, and set out to seduce her. When, after a lengthy period of indirect courtship, he made his intentions clear, she politely but firmly turned him away. In the meantime, Pierre had obtained for Beyle a substantial advancement – an appointment as commissioner for the Council of State, a prestigious post that Stendhal hoped would lead in due time to his being named a baron. His duties, which included supervision of the belongings of the imperial household and the inventory of the Napoleonic Museum, were not very taxing, leaving him ample time for reading, receptions, and the theater. Still, he was longing for something else and requested a leave in order to visit Italy again.

By the time he made this return trip, he had undertaken a massive project of reading, studying, and writing. He had immersed himself in English empirical philosophy, the French Enlightenment, and, especially while in Marseilles, the work of contemporary French empirical thinkers, in particular Destutt de Tracy. This serious philosophical work, undertaken at the same time that he was reading numerous memoirs and continuing to read extensively in creative literature, was intended to give him the insights into human nature that would permit him to become a great writer. In 1801 he had begun writing a journal – an activity he would pursue, though not continuously, until around 1815. This journal was his attempt to know himself and to understand human nature. While the journal does record facts and anecdotes, it concentrates on self-exploration and -analysis. Its timid and proud writer seeks to understand the remotest of his motivations, hoping to remain lucid in the analysis of his love affairs and his desire for fame. He knows himself to be hypersensitive yet realizes that he must hide his sensitivity from others, lest he be ridiculed, and so adopts in public the persona of a hardened cynic. Convinced that one cannot write about happiness, he concentrates on his anxieties and concerns, although there are moments, such as during his trip to Italy in 1811, when he appears relaxed in his description of the countryside, museums, theaters, churches and people.

In addition to this recording of his daily life in its intimacy, Stendhal also kept, especially from 1802 to 1805, some other notebooks which were first published in 1931 under the titles *Pensées* (Thoughts) and *Filosofia Nova* (New Philosophy). These notebooks, which represent a continued probing of human nature, are different from Stendhal's *Journal* (published posthumously in 1888) in that they concentrate on his intellectual life; they consist of notes, reactions to readings, literary projects, and drafts of articles. In a sense, they are a record of his reflections on literature broadly defined, as Stendhal seeks some kind of method through his readings that would permit him to become a great writer. The notebooks called *Filosofia Nova*, which draw from his readings of Hobbes, were intended as a philosophical treatise that would bring together all he had discovered about human nature. They can be seen as a sourcebook for many of the ideas that Stendhal would propound in his later works, such as the relativity of tastes and the dominating role of convention in society and the arts.

This notebook-keeping exercise was meant as a preparation for play-writing. From the age of 16 until his early forties, Stendhal worked and reworked various theatrical projects with the ambition of becoming the Molière of the nineteenth century. His drafts and fragments contain several attempts at tragedy and numerous attempts at comedy – none particularly original in subject matter or technique. Two plays demanded most of his attention: *Les Deux Hommes* (The Two Men), designed to show the superiority of a philosophical education (in the eighteenth-century sense), and *Letellier*, about an attempt to pervert public opinion into accepting despotism. But Stendhal was not able to bring these or any other of his plays to a successful completion. His notes and drafts show him incessantly analyzing his characters, deliberating on every move that they make. He is constantly revising the profile of his characters, parts of the plot, and sometimes the endings. We see a highly self-conscious writer unsure of his own instincts.

While he had greatly matured intellectually by the time he arrived in Milan in September 1811, Stendhal was still focused on Angela Pietragrua, with whom he had fallen in love a decade earlier. When he first presented himself to her, she did not recognize him, but after two weeks they were lovers. This was to be a brief and stormy romance. Angela was a willful and capricious woman and a consummate actress. She knew that Beyle was not her match and concocted all kinds of impediments and secret meetings that only inflamed his love further. When she ordered him to leave town for a few weeks, he complied, using the occasion to visit a number of Italian cities. Soon, his leave was over, and he had to return to France.

By the end of November he was back in Paris, working as a government administrator but, as always, bored with the work. The following July he sought and received the mission of bringing ministerial portfolios to the emperor who by then was in Russia. Thus began an adventure that was to mark him for life. He witnessed the burning of Smolensk and then of Moscow. Placed in charge of provisions for the French troops in Smolensk, he was also given the assignment of leading the retreat of 1,500 wounded soldiers from Moscow to Smolensk, 240 miles away. The trek was difficult and the convoy was under attack several times. His bravery, resourcefulness, and coolheadedness in the situation have been attested to by others. On the return to Paris later that year, he expected a decoration or promotion of some kind, but for reasons that are not clear, he did not receive the expected awards.

What Stendhal derived from this experience was a different vision of human nature. Although he was acquainted with military life and now had considerable experience as a civilian administrator, Beyle still seemed to see human life through the grid of his readings. He had still believed in honor, selflessness, and heroism. What he witnessed in Moscow and on the retreat to France were soldiers who were dishonorable, cowardly, and self-seeking. Defeat, hunger, and fear – especially fear of death – do not always bring out the best in people, and he was not prepared for that. The Enlightenment philosophes he had admired for so long were not in a position to help him cope with this experience. Their cold, rationalistic psychol-

ogy seemed totally beside the point in the face of ruthlessness and
the instinct of self-preservation.

Physically and morally drained, he could not, on his return to
Paris, interest himself in reading, writing, or love. He complained
that his energies were depleted, yet he was ordered to Germany to
manage the civil administration of the region around Sagan. Although
he seems to have handled his duties capably, once again, he fell ill
and was granted a sick leave. Returning to Milan in September 1813,
he renewed his relationship with Angela Pietragrua. The French
empire was crumbling, however, and Milan expected an imminent
invasion. It seemed incumbent on Beyle not to stay there, and he
returned to Paris only to be ordered to his native Dauphiné to assist
in organizing the defense of the region against an impending attack.
He worked valiantly, but still feeling ill, he returned to Paris in time
to witness the evacuation of the city by the Imperial family and the
arrival of the foreign occupying troops. His high hopes for a career
in Napoleon's administration were now dashed. With the emperor's
abdication, Stendhal's protector, Count Pierre Daru, no longer had
any position or influence. Stendhal lost no time in pledging
allegiance to the new royal government and found himself a new
protector in Count Jacques-Claude Beugnot. Through him, Stendhal
assiduously sought a government post from the Bourbons, hoping
that perhaps he might be given a consulate in Italy. Beugnot did
nominate him for such a position and might have succeeded in
obtaining something for him, but Beyle, disappointed at receiving
nothing and tired of waiting, once more took off for Milan where, he
thought, he might stay for good.

In the midst of all this, he had completed his first book, *Vies de
Haydn, Mozart, et de Métastase* (*The Lives of Haydn, Mozart, and
Metastasio*), which appeared in January 1815. It is certainly no surprise that Stendhal's first book should be on music, for, since his
arrival in Italy in 1801, music had been and would remain one of his
most consistent passions. Yet this is a curious work. The first, and
longest, section – that dealing with Haydn – is largely plagiarized
from Giuseppi Carpani's *Le Haydine*, published a few years earlier in
Italy. Not only does Stendhal borrow factual material and the structure of the book (in the form of letters) from Carpani, but he also
attributes to himself Carpani's analyses, judgments, and anecdotes,
going so far as to give himself a fever that Carpani had had in Vienna.

The sections on Mozart and Metastasio are also plagiarized, though less blatantly. The "Letter on Mozart," an eight-page essay, is entirely Stendhal's, however, as is the last chapter of the book, "Letter on the Present State of Music in Italy," in which he places Italian music above French music. When Carpani, the one most heavily plagiarized, protested in the press, Stendhal shamelessly accused Carpani of being the one who had plagiarized him.

The pseudonym he used to publish the book, Louis-Alexandre-César Bombet (combining the first names of three rulers with a ridiculously sounding roturian surname), should indicate that he was not taking the affair all that seriously. Richard N. Coe has proposed, however, that this is an important text for understanding Stendhal's esthetics since Stendhal found formulated in Carpani ideas he already held and would propound for quite some time, especially the notion that the pleasure caused by music is physical and the idea that the ability to appreciate certain aspects of art changes from country to country. Other ideas usually thought to be "Stendhalian," such as the assertion that German music is based on harmony while Italian music is based on melody, are drawn directly from Carpani.[1] Indeed, Stendhal and Carpani, though poles apart in character and disposition, had very similar views on music. Moreover, Stendhal is not slavish to his published sources, adding a number of comments and perspectives of his own, increasing Mozart's stature and decreasing Gluck's, for example. In the sections on Mozart and Metastasio, his manner of presentation and style are more lively and readable than those of his sources. If the book was a first opportunity for Stendhal to formulate aspects of his relativist esthetics, it was nonetheless a failure commercially.

The Milan Years

Henri Beyle was to live in Milan for seven years, interrupted by various trips to other parts of Italy and by some trips to France, mostly on family business and including, on one of the latter trips, a short visit to England. His first intent on arriving in Italy was to renew his relationship with Angela Pietragrua. She did take him back, but, alleging her husband's jealousy, she once again engaged in theatrics and banned him from Milan for prolonged periods. Only after a disenchanted maid allowed him to witness Angela's infidelity did he finally end the relationship. He later acknowledged what should have been evident at the time – that she was a "sublime strumpet."

In the two years or so following the end of his relationship with Angela, Beyle, for one of the few periods of his adult life, was not in love. He continued to read intensely; visited museums in Milan and elsewhere in Italy; spent many evenings at La Scala, which featured some of the best opera and ballet in Italy; and struck up acquaintances with most of the major writers of northern Italy as well as some who were passing through, such as Lord Byron. It is at this time that he discovered the *Edinburgh Review*, a journal that for many years was a constant source of intellectual nourishment for him. Most of the Italian writers he knew were involved in promoting Romanticism, which they defined as a literature attuned to the times. He was very much caught up in this literary ferment and even considered joining in the polemics surrounding the controversy. He also met and become friendly with liberal activists of the region and, gradually, with the Carbonari, members of the secret revolutionary society that sought to overthrow the Austrian occupation of northern Italy and unify all the Italian states.

It is perhaps through his politically minded friends that Stendhal met Mathilde Dembowski. Mathilde, whom Stendhal referred to as Métilde, had been married at 17 to a Polish military officer 20 years her senior and with whom she had had two sons but from whom she was legally separated. She was 28 when Beyle met her and by that time deeply involved in the liberal political movement. To him, she was an exquisite Lombard beauty endowed with a brilliant mind and a highly developed sensitivity. He quickly fell deeply in love with her. Although he would many times wonder whether she might have been in love with him, there is no indication that in fact she was. He declared himself early on, very delicately, and continued to do so orally and in very touching letters. She did not respond to his entreaties and, after he foolishly followed her to Volterra, where she had gone to visit her sons, she restricted him to one visit every two weeks. The pain he suffered from this unrequited love seems very real indeed, and it is clear that Mathilde, more than any woman he loved, is the one who most marked him.

By 1821 Stendhal's funds were beginning to run low, and his presence in Milan was becoming uncomfortable, for someone had spread a rumor that he was a French spy. Some of his acquaintances stopped speaking to him, and the invitations to receptions and dinners declined sharply. On the other side of the political spectrum, the Austrian authorities suspected him of being a dangerous liberal, perhaps in league with the Carbonari. They had begun to crack down harshly on the Carbonari in the Milan area, making numerous arrests. Some of Stendhal's friends fled the country, and even Mathilde was suspect to the authorities. Deeply depressed at Mathilde's continual refusal of his love, financially troubled, and politically vulnerable, Stendhal very reluctantly decided to return to France.

Stendhal's seven-year stay in Milan had been a productive one, however, for he had completed three books during this time. The first of these, *Histoire de la peinture en Italie* (*The History of Italian Painting*; actually a partial history of the Florentine school), published in 1817, draws heavily from other works, primarily from Luigi Lanzi's book in Italian by the same title. During his visit to Italy in 1811, Stendhal had purchased a copy of Lanzi's treatise and, on his return to Paris, had decided to publish a translation of it. The project soon developed into much more than a translation as Stendhal began adding his own views and commentaries and delving into other sources as well. He had already written a good deal when he left for Moscow in 1812, but in the retreat from Moscow 12 manuscript volumes he had with him were lost. It was only in 1814, when he was back in Milan, that he began rewriting the book that was published in 1817. Its author was identified only as M.B.A.A., which most scholars agree stands for "Monsieur Beyle, ancien auditeur," a reference to his final position as commissioner in the last years of the Napoleonic empire.

While this book, like his first, met with no success, it is not without interest for understanding Stendhal's esthetics. In this book Stendhal emphasizes the importance of environment – that is, climate and institutions – on art, which he sees as a product of time and place. Fidelity to his times and to himself and, of course, his sensitivity to love are, in Stendhal's judgment, among the most important qualities in an artist. Stendhal was neither knowledgeable nor interested in the technical aspects of painting. When commenting on painting, he is prone to emphasize psychology, to read a painting the way one would read a story – an approach that served him well in his descriptions of da Vinci's *Last Supper* and Michelangelo's Sistine Chapel, a description that Delacroix very much admired.

About a month after the appearance of *The History of Italian Painting*, Stendhal's third book, *Rome, Naples et Florence en 1817* (*Rome, Naples, and Florence in 1817*) appeared, the first to do so under the pseudonym Stendhal. The narrator, a German cavalry officer, proposes to guide potential tourists through his favorite Italian spots. The book could therefore be seen as a travel guide, a genre then still in its infancy. Its narrator, however, is not interested only in paintings, statues, and buildings but also, and perhaps especially, in mores. As he travels about Italy (the title, chosen by his publisher, is misleading, since other parts of Italy – Milan and Bologna especially – are treated) with a group of companions, he laces his narrative with anecdotes designed to give the reader a sense of what it means to be an Italian in the period after the Congress of Vienna. As he tells stories, engages in conversations with others, and attends concerts and operas, the narrator is also weaving a cultural and political message. Italians are living under tyranny and would be better served by a constitutional government with a bicameral legislature. Since there is currently no liberty in Italy, and since happiness cannot therefore be found in the public sector, it is found in sentiments and the arts. The life-style of the Italians is a product of their own history and their current situation. What he admires about them is that they are still, despite everything, going about the business of seeking happiness. They remain an energetic people, given to impulse and instincts. The concept of national character traits, much in disfavor today, was given of nineteenth-century thought. Stendhal used his assessment of Italian character as an indirect attack on what he perceived as the effete, conventional mores of his fellow Frenchmen.

Unlike his two previous books, this one is not heavily indebted to other published sources. He does draw some material from the *Edinburgh Review* and from Charles de Brosses, Madame de Staël, and others, but most of the material is garnered from his own experience and his own invention. Its commercial success spurred Stendhal to prepare a new edition, which appeared nine years later, in 1826. This is more than a revision or expansion of the previous book, for it incorporates only about a quarter of the material of the 1817 edition. While the format and the thematic interests are the same, it is more relaxed and witty. As with the previous book, most of the dialogues and meetings recounted are fictitious.

The other book from this period is directly related to Stendhal's love for Mathilde. As his love for her continued to go unanswered, he attempted to write a novel about their relationship but was unable to transfer his intense emotion to fiction. At the end of December 1819, however, he conceived the idea of a book on love that would be analytical in approach and would thereby provide him with the distance he had been unable to achieve in his attempt to write a novel. He completed the project, titled, appropriately, *De l'Amour (On Love)*, in six months.

The book, published in 1822, is considerably more original than *Rome, Naples, and Florence*. Beneath an appearance of detailed analysis can be detected the author's intimately personal experiences. Donning various masks and pseudonyms, Stendhal uses this book to speak about romantic love as he understands it, making now and then veiled references to his own relationship with Mathilde. A number of critics have noted a tension in the book between tenderness and dryness[2] as its author oscillates between his tender memories of Mathilde and his attempt to write a scientific, analytical book on the greatest of human emotions. Stendhal admits to this tension in chapter 9, which is only three sentences long and by that fact attracts attention to itself. The entire chapter consists of the following revealing passage: "I'm making every possible effort to remain *dry*. I'm trying to impose silence on my heart which believes it has much to say. I'm always trembling that I may have written but a sigh when I believe that I have noted a truth" (*OL*, 1: 47). The reader is much aware that the heart has not been silenced.

On Love has become famous for its formulation of passionate love and the theory of crystallization. Stendhal proposes that there are four different classifications of romantic love. The first is passionate love (*amour-passion*), that great all-encompassing passion Heloise and Abelard felt for each other. The second is love based on social tastes and played according to social rules. The third is physical love. The fourth is love inspired by vanity, reflecting the sentiments of a man who desires a fashionable woman as a luxury that he can show off. It quickly becomes evident that Stendhal is less interested in the last three categories and that what really interests him is passionate love. While passionate love cannot, like the other forms of romantic love, be abstracted from the cultures in which it is found, it retains in all of its contexts the ability to take control of the person in its throes. It is the greatest and highest of human emotions.

Love also goes through stages, seven of them, beginning with the first, admiration. These stages are not without some arbitrariness, but stage 5, crystallization, is an original contribution in its formulation, if not in conception. It purports to explain the transformation that inevitably occurs in the loved one as seen by the lover. In Stendhal's understanding of the process, the person loved takes on numerous positive characteristics in the eyes of the lover much as a branch becomes covered with crystals if left for a time in a salt mine. In love, reality is made to conform to the desires of the lover, and imagination becomes primary. The fantasizing that accompanies love is more pleasurable than the consummation of that love. *On Love* is a testimony to the power of this phenomenon.

On Love has sometimes been hailed as an early feminist treatise. There are, to be sure, some very progressive ideas on the status of women in this book in which Stendhal places himself squarely in favor of reform. He is totally opposed to forced marriages which he considered "legal prostitution" (*OL*, 1:85), arguing that "it is certainly a greater offense against decency to go to bed with a man that one has seen only twice, after three Latin words pronounced in a church, than it is to yield in spite of oneself to a man that one has been adoring for two years" (*OL*, 1:86). He favors divorce on the grounds that "the faithfulness of women in marriage when there is no love is probably against nature" (*OL*, 2:103). And he very much favors the education of women, countering the argument that instruction is harmful to women with the assertion that "the acquisition of ideas produces the same effects, both good and bad, in both sexes" (*OL*, 2:84). Stendhal needs to be given credit for expressing ideas that, while not original to him, were certainly not in the mainstream of thought in the 1820s. Yet it would be to misread him to see in him a proponent of a status for women that would be equal in all respects to that of men. One of the reasons for his desire for women who are better educated and freer to choose in love is that these kinds of women make better lovers.

The book's importance is that under the guise of a treatise it is a fascinating compendium of Stendhal's understanding of love as well as other subjects (e.g., music, literature, and mores) as they are affected by or contribute to love. Much of his analyses could be transposed to his fictional characters. Most of all, however, they relate to his love for Mathilde, for this book is her book. As he corrected the proofs, he could not help weeping, and when, in 1825, he learned of Mathilde's death, he wrote in his copy of *On Love* (in English, as he sometimes did for the most intimate of his thoughts), "Death of the Author." *On Love* remained, throughout his life, his favorite of his books.

Paris, 1821-1830

Stendhal arrived in Paris in June 1821, as despondent as he had ever been and haunted by thoughts of suicide. At first he avoided his old friends and acquaintances, fearing that they might discover his unrequited love for Mathilde. Slowly, though, he did resume a social life, renewing his old friendship with Baron de Mareste and developing a new friendship for a young writer named Prosper Mérimée. Mathilde still obsessed him, however. When his friends, thinking that they would distract him from his obvious depression, set up a party with a prostitute, he found that he could not perform sexually because he could not get Mathilde out of his thoughts. It took a five-week trip to England, during which he enjoyed the theater and the company of an engaging young prostitute, before he could resume living normally.

On his return to Paris he attended to shoring up his finances. A small annuity from his grandfather's estate and a small government pension were just barely enough for him to live on and clearly did not provide the means to live in the fashion that he liked. Luckily, he was able to do a considerable amount of journalistic writing for British publications. Beginning in 1822 and for about six years, he wrote regularly for a number of English magazines, reporting on French literature, politics, and mores. A few years later he would also write for some French publications, reviewing among other things the art salon of 1824 and various performances of the Royal Italian Theater for *Le Journal de Paris*.

Most of his articles consisted of book reviews, but they were laced with information about contemporary French culture. Stendhal was now in a good position to report on French society, for he had gained access to a number of fashionable salons, where he encountered most of the people that mattered in the arts and literature. He gained a reputation as a brilliant conversationalist, but also as a highly cynical, irreverent, acerbic, and sometimes vulgar individual. We know from his own correspondence and private papers for this period that this was in part a cover for a sensitivity that he did not want anyone to guess. At first it was a way to mask his inner anguish at his failure to win over Mathilde, but gradually he seems to have continued the facade as a way to protect his inner feelings and perhaps also because he truly enjoyed travestying himself in this manner.

One of his journalistic articles, on Rossini, led in 1823 to his second book on music, *Vie de Rossini* (*The Life of Rossini*). Despite its title, the book contains very little biographical information. Like most of his other books of nonfiction, *The Life of Rossini* is about Stendhal's own likes, dislikes, impressions, and opinions. The book, moreover, has an agenda. Stendhal had discovered Rossini's music in Italy in 1814, although he was not enthralled by it and considered it far inferior to Mozart's. When he returned to France in 1821, interest in Rossini was on the rise, and his repertoire was increasingly being performed in Paris despite the hostility of part of the musical establishment. That hostility, it seems, increased Stendhal's appreciation of Rossini, and he decided to defend him as a herald of a new music more appropriate to the times than the boring work of Ferdinand Paër and Simon Mayer that established critics seemed to prefer. Stendhal was well-placed to write about Rossini for a French audience since he was familiar with the Italian opera scene and probably knew Rossini's work better than anyone else in France. Moreover, he had gleaned a number of anecdotes about Rossini during his long stay in Italy.

After a lengthy introduction surveying European music in the early nineteenth century, the book consists of a chapter on each of Rossini's operas up to 1819. These essays are a combination of plot summary, anecdotes on the particular opera's composition, comments on audience reception, and personal reactions and impressions. Stendhal, who did not have any technical or professional expertise in music, reveals himself once again a brilliant dilettante. He does not place Rossini among the very best (Mozart and

Domenico Cimarosa occupy that position in his pantheon), but he considered him the best composer of his times and the person called on to destroy the prestige of the old music. If Rossini is incapable of lifting his listeners to the sublime, his lightness and brilliance are delightful and his music always pleasurable. The book seems to have had some success, and for the rest of the century it continued to be used by amateurs as a readable guide to Rossini and his work.

It was about this time that Stendhal also enjoyed a brief reputation as a pamphleteerist. While in Italy, he had become very interested in the debate over Romanticism and had drafted three pamphlets in support of the Romantics there, which he did not, however, publish. In October 1822 and January 1823 he published articles on the subject in the *Paris Monthly Review*. These became the first and second chapters of *Racine et Shakespeare* (*Racine and Shakespeare*), a pamphlet that appeared in 1823. After a harsh speech by a leading member of the French Academy attacking Romanticism in 1824, Stendhal returned to battle with a second pamphlet entitled, appropriately, *Racine and Shakespeare No. II*.

What had first stirred his anger was an incident in Paris in 1822 when a troupe of British actors performing Shakespeare in English was met with disruptive jeers and insults requiring police intervention. He was particularly disturbed because those preventing the performance of Shakespeare were French liberals who were using the occasion to manifest their political hostility toward England. In these pamphlets Stendhal proposes Shakespeare as a preferred model to Racine and attacks the French Academy, the unities, the requirement that serious theater be in verse, the preference for ancient subject matter over modern, and governmental censorship. His intended audience, however, seems not to be the conservatives but the liberals of his time, most of whom were supporters of neoclassicism and whom he wished to place face to face with their contradictions. Part of his strategy is to demonstrate that support for neoclassicism plays into the hands of political conservatism. He does this by closely associating the great neoclassical writers, Racine and Molière especially, with the ancien régime so despised by liberals. He further proposes dramatic subjects intended to stimulate the fervor of liberals but likely to be censored by the government. Censorship is a means for the monarchy to maintain its power. But are liberals not engaging in censorship as well? The willingness of liberals to disrupt Shakespeare is, for him, a sign that liberalism, tolerant in theory, becomes in practice a kind of tyranny. The theatrical prohibitions of the liberals and the censorship of the establishment overlap in the mentality of compulsion that motivates them. For Stendhal, the freedom of literature must take precedence over political sympathies. Both pamphlets are directed against the use of politics for the constraint of the arts. Freeing the arts will, in his judgment, lead to arts that respond to contemporary mores and tastes. Hence his definitions of Romanticism and classicism: "Romanticism is the art of presenting to peoples those literary works which, in the current state of their mores and beliefs, are susceptible of giving them the greatest pleasure possible. Classicism, on the contrary, presents to them the literature which gave the most pleasure possible to their great-grandfathers" (*RS*, 39).

A third pamphlet, *D'un nouveau complot contre les industriels* (*Concerning a New Plot against Industrialists*; 1825), also called for the freedom of the arts, this time from economic power. The pamphlet is directed against the Saint-Simonians, whose newspaper, *Le Producteur*, was, in Stendhal's reading of it, constantly singing the praises of the industrial class and proposing that economic productivity was the measure according to which all things must be judged. Stendhal counters that while industrialists do contribute to the public good, they do so consequent to their private good. That attention to private good leads them to act in a moral vacuum. Stendhal takes industrialists to task for lending to governments without regard as to whether the money is used for good or ill. He was offended by what he considered the pretensions of a group that considered itself more important to the welfare of the state than any other group. Scathingly attacking the perverted code of ethics and the pusillanimity of industrialists, Stendhal comes to the defense of writers and political leaders who do not fit the utilitarian logic of the Saint-Simonians.

The income his writings now generated permitted him to take a four-and-a-half month trip to Italy, but a more important event was the new love affair that awaited him on his return in the spring of 1804. He had known Clémentine Curial since she was in her teens, for he had been an habitué of her mother's house. Clémentine, an attractive, strong-minded, and impetuous woman who was now unhappily married, began to turn her affections toward him and took the initiative of declaring her love. For two years, they waged a tempestuous affair, reveling in secret encounters and exchanging numerous letters bristling with high passion. Clémentine, though, lost interest in Stendhal and turned to an officer on her husband's staff. Disconsolate, Stendhal considered suicide. What seems to have saved him was the decision to write his first novel, *Armance*, a story about impossible love in which the hero does commit suicide.

The publication of *Armance* (as well as a second edition of *Rome, Naples, and Florence*) in 1827 was followed by another trip to Italy, this time for six months. On his return to Paris, however, he was nearly penniless. The English magazines were no longer paying him, and his government pension, small to begin with, had been cut in half. He desperately tried, through influential friends, to obtain some governmental post. For a while it seemed that he might be given the position of librarian at the Royal Library, but this came to naught. Since his *Rome, Naples, and, Florence* had been his one really successful book, he decided to write a sequel as a way of obtaining some badly needed cash. With his cousin, Romain Colomb, helping him in his research, he was able in 1829 to publish *Promenades dans Rome* (*Walks in Rome*).

The book's ostensible purpose is to assist travelers in understanding the art, architecture, history, politics, and mores of Rome. Stendhal pretends to have written these walks the very day that they were taken, after he got back to his room in the evening, but the book was written in Paris and is actually a digest of numerous literary sources and his own accumulated knowledge about Rome. It includes many notes that Stendhal had taken but not used for *Rome, Naples, and Florence*. To give the book the flavor of having been written on the spot, Stendhal invents some traveling companions, both male and female, for whom he is an unofficial tour guide. Since he relates their opinions and reactions as well as his own, he is fictionally creating different perspectives on the various aspects of Rome, which he is explaining to his readers.

Walks in Rome differs, then, from previous guides of Rome by being totally unsystematic. Its tone is conversational and its narrator not immune from digression. He frequently talks about himself (though often apologizing for doing so) and his own tastes, which he sometimes analyzes for the reader. He reveals his fascination with acts of criminality, and his anticlericalism is blatant. Yet although he has his own strong likes and dislikes, he preaches an openness in the appreciation of the arts. A theme of his tours through Rome is that each individual should praise what he likes, not what he has been told that he ought to like. He is anxious regarding the state of the arts, though, fearing that as modern societies become obsessed with budgets and petty politics, an atmosphere will be created that will not be conducive to artistic creation.

The year 1829 was also notable for another trip, which included a visit to Barcelona, a stop in Grenoble, and a stay in Marseilles where Stendhal conceived the idea of a novel that would become *Le Rouge et le Noir* (*The Red and the Black*). On his return to Paris he set about to write some short stories and to complete this novel. He also struck up another amorous relationship, this time with Giulia Rinieri, an aristocratic Italian woman whom he had known for some time. She made clear her interest in him, and a serene, gentle love seems to have developed between them. During his relationship with Giulia and while he was correcting the proofs for *The Red and the Black*, the revolution of 1830 broke out in Paris. The fall of the Bourbons and the advent of a more liberal regime renewed his hopes for government employment. Again he was assisted by his many friends, some of them with influence. He had wanted a prefecture, but when it became clear that one would not be forthcoming, he asked for a consulate. He was offered the consulate at Trieste, a city he did not know, but accepted immediately. Before leaving for his new post, he wrote to Giulia's guardian asking for her hand in marriage. At age 47 he seems to have genuinely wanted the stability that a marriage with Giulia would afford. The guardian was polite in his response, but asked for more time.

The Consular Years, 1831-1842

Stendhal arrived at his post in Trieste at the end of November 1830. His position as consul had not, however, yet been accepted by the Austrian authorities. While waiting for that approval he began exercising some of the functions of his office and took the opportunity to travel to Fiume and Venice. On 24 December he received the news that the Austrian government had refused to accept his nomination. Since this same government had expelled him from Milan as politically dangerous, it is not surprising that it did not want him as

France's representative in one of its territories. Stendhal, again with the help of his friends, sought a reassignment and was posted to Civitavecchia, a small, unattractive town, though the main port of the Papal States. Moreover, his salary as consul in Civitavecchia was one-third less than the posting in Trieste brought. The Papal government, as unhappy as the Austrians about having him on its territory, expressed its displeasure but was reluctant to risk its relations with the new French government over the affair. It accepted Beyle's nomination, but kept him under surveillance.

All the evidence available suggests that Stendhal did a competent and conscientious job as French consul, but he found Civitavecchia increasingly unbearable and, whenever possible, traveled to Rome where he could find music, theater, and good conversation. He tried to occupy himself with writing, composing in 1831 *Mémoires d'égotisme* (*Memoirs of Egotism*), an autobiographical piece covering his years in Paris in the 1820s. Giulia Rinieri was now living in Sienna, and Stendhal had not totally given up hope that his marriage proposal might somehow be accepted. He made a number of trips to Sienna in 1832-33, and it appears that they were able to resume their intimacy. Marriage, however, was not in the cards for Stendhal, for Giulia was soon married off to a distant relative. He then appears to have proposed marriage to another woman whose identity, however, is unclear. There were other trips, to Florence in particular and, in the fall of 1833, a three-month leave in Paris during which he was able to renew his active social and cultural life.

By this time the Foreign Ministry was becoming increasingly unhappy with Stendhal's frequent absences from his post and made it clear that it expected him to remain in Civitavecchia. Stendhal reluctantly complied, and these were among the most miserable years of his life. There are constant notes in his papers about his boredom and suffering in what he referred to as "this hole." His situation was not made any better by his top aide, Lysimaque Tavernier, whom he had originally trusted and for whom he had obtained a promotion to chancellor of the consulate in 1834 but who now took every advantage to damage his superior's reputation with the ministry in Paris. Stendhal endured as best he could, in part because he had no other alternative, interesting himself in archaeological digs being undertaken in the region, occasionally hunting, and attempting to write still another novel, now known as *Lucien Leuwen*, and another autobiography. Nor had he given up the idea of marriage. This time he proposed to a young woman from a respectable family in Civitavecchia, but this too came to nothing.

Finally, in 1836 he was granted another leave that he was able to prolong over three years. He returned to Paris, renewing his old habits of attending the theater, the opera, and the various high-society drawing rooms to which he had entry. Again he sought marriage, to a widow of 46, but that too failed to materialize. Giulia was now back in Paris, and he seems to have renewed his relations with her. Meanwhile, he was working on a biography of Napoleon that he never brought to completion. A more attractive literary project was the possibility of writing another travel book, this time on France instead of Italy. From May through July he traveled in France to document the book. This firsthand knowledge, plus bookish sources and information furnished him by various friends, led to the *Mémoires d'un touriste* (*Memoirs of a Tourist*), published in 1838.

The book is narrated by an iron merchant who has spent a good part of his life in the colonies. Well-educated and cultivated, he has not let his mercantile life stifle his cultural tastes, for on his travels he attends musical performances and visits local libraries, theaters, and churches. As he travels through France (he has a particular affection for the South), he keeps a journal in which he records his impressions, commenting on architecture, hotels, and cafés, as would be expected of any travel book, but also showing a surprising interest in urban planning. He is most mostly interested in people, both town-folk and peasants, in what and how they think and feel, liberally relating anecdotes as he goes along. As can be expected, this iron merchant espouses many of the ideas we know to be Stendhal's. Stendhal had hoped that his book would be successful and, anticipating this, he took still another trip to gather information for future volumes. This material was published posthumously as a third volume of the *Memoirs of a Tourist* or separately as *Voyages dans le Midi de la France* (*Voyages in the South of France*).

In the meantime, Stendhal had begun writing short stories for the *Revue des Deux Mondes*, and in late 1838 he began his second great novel, *La Chartreuse de Parme* (*The Charterhouse of Parma*), which he would complete in about eight weeks. He also had the idea of still another novel that would have a peasant girl as its central character. This project would never reach completion and was published posthumously as *Lamiel*. There was still another trip to England, but when Stendhal's protector, Count Molé, resigned from his post as foreign minister, Stendhal had no option but to return to his consulate in Civitavecchia.

This last period in Civitavecchia, approximately two years, was one of the darkest in Stendhal's life. Lysimaque Tavernier was even more insolent than before. The city had not gotten any lovelier, and, with failing health, Stendhal found the climate more difficult to endure. Still, he seems to have made side trips to visit and perhaps renew intimacy with Giulia Rinieri, and he seems to have had one final passion about which we know little for a woman whom he names Earline. By now Stendhal's health was seriously deteriorating. He had never been of robust health, having had recurring problems with kidney stones and gout, but now he was developing clear signs of cardiovascular disease. Plagued by sudden loss of consciousness, headaches, and dizziness, he continued his functions as best he could until he suffered a stroke. He slowly recovered, though not without some signs of aphasia, but he was clearly too ill to continue, and once again he was granted a sick leave.

When Stendhal arrived in Paris in the fall of 1841, his friends were shocked at how much he had aged and how ill he looked. Paris seemed to stimulate him, however, and he renewed his social life as in the past. He worked on still more short stories and on the manuscript of *Lamiel*. On 22 March 1842, as he was walking along a Paris boulevard, he slumped to the sidewalk unconscious, felled by a major stroke. He did not regain consciousness and died early the following morning. In his will he had made his cousin, Romain Colomb, his literary executor. It was a good choice. Colomb was able to save most of the manuscripts then in Stendhal's possession and supervised a 19-volume edition of Stendhal's works, including a number of posthumous writings, which appeared in 1853-55.

Chapter Two

Armance: The Impossible Ethic

Genesis and Plot

Stendhal's first novel, *Armance* (1827), had its origin in a literary hoax. In the 1820s the Duchess de Duras had attained some celebrity through novels of impossible love. Her first novel, *Ourika* (1824), related the story of the love of a young black woman for a white Frenchman; her second, *Edouard* (1825), the love of a plebeian for an aristocrat. A third novel, *Olivier ou le secret* (Oliver, or The Secret), about the love of a young man with an unmentionable secret, had been read to friends but not published. Henri de Latouche, a writer and journalist, then seized the opportunity for some mischief and published his own novel, titled *Olivier*, featuring an impotent hero. He cleverly used the same format as Duras's previously unsigned novels, with the same announcement that proceeds would go to charity. Stendhal, who had reviewed *Olivier* for the *New Monthly Magazine* (and had also pretended that Duras was the author), decided to write his own version, and his hero's name was also to be Olivier.

The novel, then, has a definite literary context, one acknowledged by Stendhal himself and recognized by at least two reviewers at the time of publication.[1] This context suggests that *Armance* deals with impotence – a suggestion further strengthened by a letter dated 23 December 1826 that Stendhal wrote to his friend and fellow writer Prosper Mérimée. In this letter Stendhal makes clear references to Octave's sexual inadequacy. Responding to Mérimée, who had objected to Stendhal's naming the hero Olivier, Stendhal wrote, "I chose the name Olivier spontaneously because of the challenge. I insist on it because this name alone makes a statement and one that is not indecent. If I used Edmond or Paul, many people would not guess the fact of *Babilanism*" (*Corr.*, 2:96). *Babilanism* was an Italianism that meant "impotence."

The plot of the novel makes no such clear reference, however. It relates the story of Octave, a young nobleman of strange habits who harbors a secret. Despite his promise to himself never to fall in love, he does fall in love with his distant cousin, Armance. Although clearly in love with him, she refuses his love, alleging various implausible reasons. Both reveal their love to each other, however, when Octave is believed to be dying after being wounded in a duel. Yet both insist that their love will remain a pure one, never to lead to marriage. After Armance has been seen near Octave's room by their malicious uncle, Commander de Soubirane, they do agree to wed to save Armance's honor. The uncle, who opposes this marriage, however, forges a letter from Armance to her best friend in which she explains that she does not love Octave and is entering into marriage reluctantly. Octave, who finds this letter, believes it to be authentic but goes through with the marriage out of a sense of honor and duty. Shortly after the wedding he sets off for Greece, ostensibly to participate in the liberation of that country, but he commits suicide as he approaches the coast. On learning the news, Armance and Octave's mother enter a convent.

This plot, which Stendhal considered "irreprochable," has been the object of considerable criticism. Commentators have pointed out that the novel relies on several well-worn procedures, of which the counterfeit letter is but one; that it contains a number of implausibilities; and that Stendhal introduces characters solely for the purpose of advancing his plot. In this novel, however, Stendhal is not as much interested in the narration of events as he is in the exploration of characters facing personal dilemmas. His first novel devalues plot as a way of highlighting the internal drama of the characters. The number of pages devoted to their thoughts and feelings is far greater than those relating what goes on outside them. External events are typically narrated with extreme terseness while a moment of anxiety may be described for several pages. To achieve this, Stendhal relies heavily on the interior monologue, which emerges as his preferred means for penetrating into the mind of his characters and for correcting the false readings that they make of one another.

Yet even the interior monologues do not give the reader a clear notion of the nature of Octave's problem. The cause for his refusal of love and marriage is never revealed in the text. Late in the novel Octave himself begins to allude to a secret – a development that casts him in a Byronic light but only increases the mystery further. This lack of an explanation for Octave's bizarre behavior was in large part the reason for the poor reception of the novel. Stendhal's friends were unanimous in their dislike of the work. Most of its first readers professed not to understand it, with one reviewer suggesting that the author had modeled his characters after the inmates of the famous asylum at Charenton and another exclaiming that "one feels like one is walking through a madhouse."[2] Saint-Beuve summed up the reactions of his contemporaries by calling the novel "basically enigmatic."[3] This novel, which Stendhal compared to the great French classic *La Princesse de Clèves* (*The Princess of Cleves*), remains today, as Aldous Huxley once put it, "the queerest of all Stendhal's writings."[4]

The Behavioral Problem

Understandably, much of the commentary on *Armance* has attempted to explain Octave's behavior. Why does this young, handsome, intelligent, educated, wealthy aristocrat harbor such a somber disposition and why can he not seem to take pleasure in anything? Why is he given to bouts of "extreme violence" and "extraordinary maliciousness" (*A*, 35) to the extent that he would have been locked up, explains the narrator, were it not for his family's lineage? Why is he so misanthropic and why so despairing when he finds out that he is in love? The diagnosis of the doctors whom his mother has consulted is that Octave is afflicted with that familiar malady of the period, *le mal du siècle*. Their diagnosis, which has generally not been taken seriously by critics (with the exception of Roger Pearson) but which the narrator seems to accept on at least one occasion (*A*, 105), deserves some attention.

The origins of *le mal du siècle* – whose principal characteristics include melancholy, abulia, and alienation from society – are still disputed but probably extend back to Goethe's 1774 novel, *Sorrows of Young Werther*. In France the malady was associated mainly with Chateaubriand's brief 1802 novel, *René*. There are, to be sure, similarities between Chateaubriand's story and Stendhal's. The male protagonists of both texts are melancholy, narcissistic types who indulge in daydreaming, love solitude, and, more importantly, love women who resemble them. The narrator's remark that Octave "only lacked a common soul" (*A*, 41) recalls Chactas's perception that the solution to René's problem lies in his accepting a life of "common ways."[5] Octave even quotes René (without mentioning him or using quotation marks) when he says, "I am here in the midsts of a desert of men" (*A*, 108). Moreover, Chateaubriand's text, like Stendhal's, presents the reader with a hermeneutic code, with secrets to be divined. Amélie's secret is that she is in love with her brother, and René's secret may be that he harbors incestuous desires for his sister. These desires would render him incapable of the social integration that could be accomplished only through sexual integration – that is, marriage. Like Octave, René is forced to marry, but he chooses not to live with his wife.

Octave's malady, unlike René's, is devoid of metaphysical dimensions, however. There is no yearning for the absolute, no frustration with the finite in Octave, who remains impervious to Madame de Bonnivet's attempts to interest him in metaphysical issues. Nor does the text propose a religious solution to its hero's woes, as does *René*. Moreover, Stendhal's and Chateaubriand's attitudes toward their protagonists are dissimilar, with Stendhal being more ironic but less judgmental than Chateaubriand. Stendhal's narrator periodically underscores Octave's lack of lucidity regarding himself, ironically noting that he acts "without knowing why," "without noticing that he was doing it," and "without his knowing it" (*A*, 50, 51). The narrator observes that "our philosopher hadn't the slightest idea that he was in love with Armance" (*A*, 90). Octave later enjoys Armance's loving glances "without understanding them" (*A*, 134), although Armance's voice "would have informed anyone but Octave of the love she had for him" (*A*, 156). Ironically, neither his substantial readings in empirical philosophy and psychology nor his introspective monologues supply Octave with any insight into the workings of his own psyche.

If the themes of *le mal du siècle* are inscribed within the text, they are also the subject of the narrator's critique. After the publication of *René* in 1802, it had become fashionable for young nobles to appear depressed and anguished and to consider themselves deeper and more philosophical as a result. Octave is not immune from this ailment: "It is difficult to escape the malady of one's times: Octave thought himself philosophical and profound" (A, 105). He is, of course, neither. But the young men afflicted with *le mal du siècle* had, in Stendhal's eyes, no tangible cause for their melancholy. In a note in the margins of his preface to *Armance*, he wrote, "What is ridiculous about these young people and what this novel wants to warn them about is that without having Octave's misfortune, they appear as somber as he does" (A, 308). Commenting elsewhere on the relationship between Octave and the young men of his time, he wrote, "What is *ridiculous* about them is that they are as sad as he is without having the same reasons" (A, 305). Or, still more specifically, in some notes, he wrote, "Although not impotent, these young privileged men . . . are either very immature or *as* unhappy as the impotent Octave. That is what is ridiculous about them" (A, 306). That is, Octave has a reason for being melancholy; the so-called *malades du siècle* do not.

While it does shed light on the novel, *le mal du siècle* explanation does not assist the reader in learning the nature of Octave's secret nor its function in this narrative. Every commentator would agree that the secret is at best ambiguously encoded in the text. The two other major characters are aware of a mystery, but neither succeeds in deciphering it. Octave does finally reveal it to them – posthumously – but *not* to the reader. Some critics have interpreted Octave's problem as bisexuality, and certain aspects of Octave's behavior, such as his visits to brothels, could be accounted for in this reading. There were well-know contemporaries – Custine, and Girodet especially – who were reputed to be bisexual, and there may be veiled allusions to Custine in the novel.[6] If such were his condition, Octave, whose sense of duty and propriety is considerable, would have considered himself a "monster" and would certainly not have wanted to taint a marriage with this tendency.

Other critics have alluded to Octave's fixation with his mother as possibly complicating normal love relationships. The narrator does note in the first paragraph of the novel that Octave loved her "with a kind of passion" (A, 7), and Octave himself tells her in the first chapter, "I love only you on this earth" (A, 18). Other texts corroborate the greater than average intensity of Octave's love for his mother. Yet toward the end of the novel, when his love for Armance has reached a peak of intensity, "he realized with horror that he no longer loved his mother" (*A*, 192) and repeated to himself, "You no longer love your mother" (*A*, 192). Most critics, however, have offered a reading based on what is known of the novel's genesis and the contents of Stendhal's letter to Mérimée and have concluded that the secret in question is impotence. But can the conditions relating to the writing of the story and the letter Stendhal wrote to a friend after completing the novel be decisive in our reading of this novel?

The critical value of Stendhal's letter has been challenged on several levels. It has been argued that the letter to Mérimée, crude and cynical as it is, could be explained by Stendhal's well-known desire to appear as a libertine and a rake to his young friend.[7] While this would explain its vulgar tone, it need not invalidate its content, for we have, in addition to this letter, another letter – this one to Sutton Sharpe – in which the author clearly states that "the hero, Octave, is *impotens*" (*Corr.*, 2:139). Marginal comments in Stendhal's own hand also make the same revelation. Other critics, such as Shoshana Felman, have cautioned against using the letter to Mérimée on the grounds that it is an extratextual datum that should not be allowed to intrude on the reading of the novel.[8] This is a serious argument and a point well-taken – if we assume ourselves as first readers. Practically all twentieth-century editions of *Armance*, however, include the letter, so that it is difficult for anyone to approach this novel with esthetic virginity. Indeed, our first reading of *Armance* would probably resemble what Roland Barthes called a "rereading" or a "second reading."[9] Unlike Stendhal's contemporaries, most readers today would approach the text with the knowledge of Stendhal's own proposed solution to the hermeneutic code.

Prior knowledge of the secret does make of the reader a privileged decoder. Enigmatic statements by the narrator relating to Octave's hatred of love and to his tendency to exaggerate pleasures he could not enjoy now seem to have a clear referent. Moreover, a number of Octave's acts are explained: his considering the priesthood, although he clearly has no religious vocation; his flight from a performance of Scribe's *Mariage de raison* (Marriage of Convenience) when the husband is given the key to the conjugal bedroom; his frequent quarrels with his male friends; his gratuitous acts of violence. Finally, the symbolic value of his visit to Heloise and Abelard's tomb in the company of Armance becomes transparent. If we were to accept the letter to Mérimée not as outside the text but as part of the text, if we were to assume Octave's impotence, be it real or imaginary, this might explain much of Octave's behavior. Unfortunately, it does not answer a number of crucial questions.

Why should Octave's impotence be an obstacle to his having a relationship with Armance? This woman "of terrifying purity," to quote F. W. J. Hemmings,[10] is secretly in love with Octave, and her behavior, almost as bizarre as Octave's, would indicate that he could find no better partner for a nonsexual marriage. Had she not considered entering a convent to avoid revealing her love and become physically weak, then ill, when Madame de Malivert proposed that she marry Octave? Even when she became sure of his love for her, she made him promise when he seemed on the verge of death never to bring up the question of marriage and later agreed to marry him only when it became a matter of salvaging her honor and Octave's. Since she is clearly not eager for a sexual relationship, why could Octave not have proposed some kind of nonsexual arrangement to Armance?

It is clear, however, that neither character is capable of proposing any such relationship. Even if we allow that in a nineteenth-century context such a subject could not have been discussed easily, we must concur with Geneviève Mouillaud and Shoshana Felman that the crux of the problem lies in *verbal* impotence.[11] Felman's insight is that the absence of a key to the mystery within the text is itself functional: "It is not, in fact, the key that is lacking, but a lack which is the key. It is not the essential that is eluded, but the ellipsis that is essential" (Felman, 170). Felman has correctly argued that if neither the author nor the hero can bring himself to divulge the secret, it is because the secret is that which is unnamable – that is, impossible to say (Felman, 174). But why is the secret unnamable? Why is it impossible for Octave to reveal it to Armance? Why must he resort to false revelations such as claiming that he has no conscience or that he is a kleptomaniac? Armance, it must be recalled, is not too different from Octave in this respect either. She too has a secret (she is in love with Octave) and resorts to a false revelation (she claims to be betrothed to someone else) while pretending that this revelation is only partial (she will not reveal the name of her fiancé). Why do these two characters so in love with each other feel so compelled not to communicate with each other? In short, we are still faced with a behavioral problem that goes beyond the question of impotence and even beyond the question of inarticulateness. This leads us to examine the ethic that underlies the behavior.

Ethos and Action

From the beginning of the novel, the narrator has informed his readers that duty was Octave's only motivation for acting. It is even said of him that he is "duty incarnate" (*A*, 9). If Stendhal did borrow from Duras and Latouche the general idea for his novel, and from Latouche certain aspects of the plot, it is clear that the character Octave owes nothing to either Duras's or Latouche's Oliviers. The latter heroes may be partially motivated by duty, but their narrators do not emphasize this as part of their personalities. For Octave, however, all obligation is to duty, which is an end in itself, considered to be right regardless of his motives as agent or the result of its application. His sense of duty is part of a complex emotional imperative (related to his sexual anxieties, oedipal temptations, and narcissistic tendencies), but in its manifestation it clearly belongs to an ethical system that is not too dissimilar from that under which Corneille's characters operate. A monologue in the second chapter during which Octave contemplates suicide reveals the full dimensions of his sense of duty. The thought of his parents at first deters him from the possibility of taking his own life, but he decides that they do not love him anyway. These thoughts then follow: "It's a pretty light duty which binds me to them. . . . This word *duty* was like a lightning bolt for Octave. A *light duty*! he shouted . . . , a duty of so little importance! . . . Is it of such little importance if it's the only one I have left?" (*A*, 31). This is part of a refrain that will last until the end of the novel, but what is noteworthy here is that the happiness of his parents does not enter into his considerations: duty is a value in itself. In this sense Octave is quite different from his novelistic successor, Julien Sorel, for whom duty is also very important but for whom it is clearly axiological – that is, aimed at results.

Octave's concept of duty is clearly inseparable from the esteem/contempt axis that also dominated Corneille's heroes. It is significant that Octave falls in love with Armance while trying to regain her esteem after believing that she considered him to be base.

That she should think this torments him, and he considers it "essential to his honor" (A, 52) to prove differently. The narrator tells us that "he passionately desired to regain Armance's esteem" (A, 54) and that he is particularly pained because "he saw himself refused an esteem which he was certain he deserved" (A, 53). The psychological paradox this situation produces is thoroughly Cornelian: "He esteemed Armance greatly and, so to speak, uniquely; he saw that she had contempt for him and he esteemed her precisely because of this contempt" (A, 65). In equal importance to Armance's esteem for him is Octave's esteem for himself. When a jesting remark by Madame d'Aumale makes Octave suddenly realize he is in love with Armance, he is deeply grieved because "he had just lost all rights to his self-esteem. The world would be henceforth closed for him: he had not enough virtue to live in it" (A, 159). A few pages later he exclaims, "All I had was my self esteem; I've lost it" (A, 162). He is left tortured by shame, despair, and self-hatred.

If we turn to Armance, we find a moral vision that even in its verbal expression is homologous to that of Octave. It too is based on a moral elitism with nobility of soul as its center. When Octave inherits a fortune, Armance becomes obsessed at the thought that he might lose his noble soul: "She kept asking herself: Does he have a vulgar soul?" (A, 91). Although she discovers her love for him much sooner than he discovers his love for her, throughout most of the novel Armance is as opposed to marriage to Octave as he is opposed to marriage to her. The reason, ostensibly, is that it would be ignoble for her, who has no fortune, to appear to be seeking or even accepting marriage to Octave, who is wealthy. Armance thereby seems to be operating under ethical premises similar to Octave's. To wed her rich relative would make her unworthy of him, devalue her esteem in his eyes and that of society. It is thus her duty to prevent a marriage, even if it means lying and pretending that she is already betrothed. The Cornelian paradox holds: to refuse him is the only way to remain worthy of him.

We have sufficient reason to doubt, however, that the disproportion in fortunes is the sole reason that Armance is so fearful of marriage to Octave. She repeats the impediment to herself again and again and usually links it with the anticipated public condemnation of such a marriage. The knowledge that her own conduct is irreproachable is not enough: "Although her conduct was perfectly proper, she imagined that it was easy to read in her eyes when she was looking at her cousin" (*A*, 234). This is indeed what happens when some aristocratic ladies begin murmuring that Armance is positioning herself "to become Viscountess de Malivert, which wasn't bad for a young lady who was poor and of low birth" (*A*, 244). Armance is shattered when she learns this: "The idea of being calumnied to that extent had never occurred to Armance. I'm a lost woman, she said to herself; my sentiments for Octave are more than suspected, and that's not the biggest fault which they are attributing to me; I live in the same house that he does, and it's not possible that he marry me. . . . From that moment, the idea of the calumnies leveled against her, which overcame all Armance's reasoning, poisoned her life" (*A*, 244). At a point in time roughly contemporary with the preceding passage, however, Armance learns that she has inherited "a considerable fortune which would make her an acceptable party for Octave" (*A*, 245). This, we would expect, would have a major effect on her, since it would eliminate the major barrier to her marrying Octave. But the narrator informs us that this was "a development which affected her little" (*A*, 245). It is only later, after her return to Paris and in the face of Octave's indifference, that she begins to reflect on what this inheritance could have meant.

We must now turn to a second reason Armance has used for refusing to wed Octave – namely, his lack of love for her. The belief that Octave does not love her – despite all evidence to the contrary – helps to strengthen her resolve. Indeed, she needs the assurance that Octave does not love her: "She wanted to believe that Octave had no love for her; each day, she needed this certitude in order to justify in her own eyes the kind attention which her tender friendship permitted itself" (*A*, 120). Still, this same supposed lack of love on Octave's part anguishes her to the extent that at times, it renders her incapable of speaking. Yet, when Madame de Malivert assures her that Octave does love her, we learn that "these assurances of Octave's love were heart-rending for Armance" (*A*, 125). Moreover, when Octave, thinking he is on his own deathbed, admits to her that he has loved her with passion, she does not match his revelation with one of her own, despite the fact that their fortunes are no longer disproportionate. She talks about her deep friendship for him and makes him promise never to ask for her hand, should he live. Shortly afterwards, when Octave's lips "dared to touch her cheek lightly" (A, 231), Armance reacts in anger, and a two-day tiff is the result.

Armance is no longer poor; she is now assured of Octave's love. Why, then, must she go on refusing it? Even after the marriage has been agreed to by both of them (in order to save her honor), Armance, having noticed that Octave is troubled, says to him, "I have a proposal to make to you: let us return to a perfectly happy state and to that sweet intimacy which was the charm of my life, since I've known that you love me, until this fatal idea of marriage. I'll take the blame for such a bizarre change. I'll tell people that I made a vow never to marry. Such an idea will incur blame and will lower the opinion that a few friends might have of me; what do I care?" (A, 274-75). Armance had once before been willing to brave public opinion, when she had rushed to Clamart believing that Octave was dying, but the public condemnation that she feared would greet her marriage to Octave is now of no concern when it is a question of breaking up the planned marriage. Her generosity in offering Octave a way out of a marriage she is unsure he wants coheres with her own reticence toward marriage. Octave may have legitimate reasons for wishing to guard against love. But Armance? Since the only relationship envisaged for her is both moral and legal, the reader can only conclude that the reasons she has given do not go to the heart of the problem.

When thinking about her relationship with Octave, Armance typically associates it with shame when it is in the context of love and with purity when in the context of a close friendship. At one point, when she believes that for the first time her behavior may have revealed her love to him, she flees and allows herself a tearful monologue replete with charged lexical items: "shame," "horror," "the most extreme uneasiness," "despair," "honor lost," "fatal secret," "now lost," "lost forever," "without a way out," "the whole extent of my weakness," "fatal love," "dreadful passion" (A, 83-85, passim). At the end of this monologue she decides that if she is to remain worthy of Octave, she must retire to a nunnery.

That her chief desire is to be able to love Octave without the possibility of intimacy is evident from her monologue in chapter 13, after Madame de Malivert has assured her once more of Octave's love. The narrator affirms that Armance was quite resolved never to accept her cousin's hand: "I'll be able to love him secretly, . . . and

I'll be as happy and perhaps happier than if I had been his mate. Don't they say that marriage is the grave of love, that there may be pleasant marriages, but that none is delightful? I tremble at the thought of marrying my cousin. If I saw that he wasn't the happiest of men, I'd be at the height of despair. On the other hand, if we continue to live in our pure and holy friendship, none of the minor concerns of life will ever attain the heights of our sentiments and be able to tarnish them" (*A*, 127-28). In the previous chapter she had reflected that if she had a fortune that could have permitted her to marry Octave, then "he would have found more happiness with me than with any other woman in the world" (*A*, 122). This confidence is very short-lived. Her fear that somehow marriage will put an end to their love, that somehow she might not be able to make Octave happy, could be interpreted as a recognition that Octave is a troubled man, given to depressive states, but it may hide a fear that she will be unable to perform the duties of conjugal love. The "pure and holy friendship" she prefers is clearly a chaste relationship.

The sentiments of duty, honor, and esteem explain why Octave was not able to propose an asexual arrangement to Armance. He is not able, as André Gide has pointed out, to envisage marriage outside the obligations such a union entails. In contrast to his namesake in Musset's *La Confession d'un enfant du siècle (Confession of a Child of the Century)* who cannot envisage sex without love, Octave seems to be unable to come to terms with love without sex. The same might be said of Armance. Her moral code is such that she, like Octave, would consider physical love an obligation. She seems to fear that the accomplishment of this duty would destroy their happiness, and we can well imagine her speaking or thinking the words of Gide's Allissa: "I've often reflected on what our life together would have been like. As soon as it was no longer perfect, I would no longer have been able to bear . . . our love."[12] Although she, unlike Alissa, is able ultimately to conquer her fears, her sense of duty prevents her from revealing enough of her love soon enough to avoid disaster.

The paradox is that the ethos of the Cornelian world – an ethos that leads to heroism and grandeur – leads here to a dead end. The value system under which Corneille's characters operate resulted in action because the community of which they were a part – that is, the nobility – accepted their moral premises. The Cornelian hero "does not seek salvation for himself, but in the name of an Order which is valid for others."[13] He knows his attitude to be exemplary, for he knows that it transcends both himself as an individual as well as historical accidents. The Cornelian sublime was already a bit archaic under Louis XIV, but by the Restoration in the nineteenth century, no longer did the nobility no longer practice it, they did not even accept the value of its moral premises.

In the aristocratic milieu of *Armance* it is fair game to make fun of Octave's exaggerated sense of duty. The aristocracy has totally abandoned the values formerly associated with it and has replaced them with bourgeois values. Bankers are readily welcome in their midst. Mothers are interested in the newly wealthy Octave as a potential husband for their daughters – a fact Octave finds thoroughly revolting. He is shocked that aristocrats "dare flaunt such an adoration of money in one of the most distinguished drawing rooms of France, whose members could not open a history text without coming across a hero bearing their name" (*A*, 29). Yet Octave's uncle, Commander de Soubirane, who turns out to be the villain of the novel, urges his nephew to play the stock market to augment his wealth even further.

These nobles have not, for their conversion to the values of capitalism, become more forward-looking. In a sense Octave is more modern than they, since he was educated at the progressive Polytechnic School and is well-versed in empirical philosophy. The aristocracy in *Armance* would reject the modern world in order to restore the feudal world without the latter's values. Octave and Armance, in their disdain for money, are the novel's true aristocrats. They reject the money-centered values of the modern world, preferring to adhere to feudal values while aware that the end of the aristocracy is near. They lucidly compare themselves to pagan priests on the eve of the triumph of Christianity. For them, the concept of the aristocracy has moral dimensions; as exceptions to the moral bastardization of the aristocracy, they are anachronisms.

Whereas the coincidence of social conditions and moral conditions in the Cornelian universe made heroic action possible, the discrepancy between the social conditions of life in the Restoration salons and the archaic moral code of Octave means that Octave's ethical attitude can be exemplary for himself only. His attempts to attach his conduct and his values to the universal construct of reason fail, for reason cannot assuage his continued distress. His ethic leads not to a willful energy but to self-repression, to an effort to become sufficient unto himself. He is left with his self-defined and self-defining duty, an aristocratic Narcissus yearning for a bedroom with large mirrors.

Love might have provided a way out of this self-preoccupation. Octave seems to realize this early in the novel when he reflects that his only recourse in the face of the general degradation around him "would be to find a beautiful soul . . . , and attach myself to her forever, see only her, live with her and only for her and her happiness. I would love her with passion" (*A*, 30). Indeed, Octave's madness diminishes as he permits love to gain an ascendency (Felman, 167). But love, precisely, cannot triumph. Perhaps Octave has raised Armance – whose initials, A.Z., recall alpha and omega, the joint symbols of God as the beginning and end of all things – to too high a level. He clearly fears her judgment as one would of a god: "Armance has always frightened me. I have never been able to approach her without feeling that I was appearing before the master of my destiny" (*A*, 297). That he considers her so fearsome a judge is an impediment to their relationship.

A more important impediment lies in his inability to overcome his own predisposed enmity toward passion and love – something Armance does succeed in doing. Contempt for passion and even vows never to fall in love are characteristics, we might note, of Byronic heroes,[14] although no reader has been tempted to consider Byron's heroes impotent. Beyond the Byronic allusions, then, we are dealing with a more troubling aversion to love. Here the patent symbolism of Octave's family name comes into play. At one point his uncle, in a rare moment of lucidity, refers to Octave's "soul so pure that it is frozen" (*A*, 9). Octave's last name, Malivert, is nearly homophonous with *"mal d'hiver"* – the ailment of winter. But "Malivert/*mal d'hiver*" could also – by analogy with other expressions such as *"mal du pays"* – refer to a yearning for winter, a yearning for frigidity, for a state in which passion does not exist. For passion, whatever his will might decide, cannot be suppressed. His deepest impotence, as Eric Gans has put it, "is not his inability to desire, but rather his inability to resist desire."[15]

The *morale de grandeur*, having no outlet in nineteenth-century society, has degenerated into a form of narcissism. The passage in which Octave envisages the possibility of salvation through love is not too far removed from René's ultimately solipsistic wish that he find a woman so like himself that she be "an Eve taken from myself" (René, 160). Octave loves in Armance that which is like him[16] and projects on her the same kinds of judgments he would make on himself. Felman has pointed out the importance of the scene where Octave is on the point of revealing himself to Armance. Telling her that he will reveal his secret, he looks at Armance "not as a lover, but in order to see what she would think" (A, 276). Octave is thinking of the effect of his revelation before saying it. How he will appear in Armance's eyes is most important. Earlier in the novel he had admitted that "my pride raises a wall of diamond between me and other men" (A, 150). Octave is never fully engaged in either thought or action. He is incapable of total absorption in anything, for he cannot free thought or activity from self-preoccupation. For him, consciousness is not possible without self-consciousness. He had, the narrator tells us early in the novel, "the habit of always trying to judge the amount of happiness he was experiencing at the moment" (A, 53). Rather than think or act, he is reduced to thinking of himself thinking or to thinking of himself acting. His "imperious need to see another Viscount de Malivert in action" (A, 150) projects the need to contemplate himself a step further.

Octave must live according to an ethical image of himself that is uncompromising. Unable to fulfill the terms of a marriage he has had to contract to save Armance's honor, he must kill himself so that his noble image of himself might persist. Perken's comment to Claude in André Malraux's La Voie royale (The Royal Way), 1930, applies perfectly well to Octave: "He who kills himself is chasing after an image that he has formed of himself: you never kill yourself except to exist."[17] The act of suicide, like Octave's other acts, is ethically non-teleological: its rightness or wrongness is not definable in terms of its consequences. Even in death, his ethical attitude remains deonto-logical, for he surely knows that the prime consequence of his sui-cide will be to inflict pain on Armance and his mother. On this point, the difference with the Cornelian hero is striking. Corneille's heroes, though frequently obsessed with the idea of killing themselves or having themselves killed for honor's sake, never actually do. This may be because in Corneille's world a heroic action of any kind is exemplary. Octave's death on the shores of Greece cannot be considered exemplary at all, except in the sense that it forces on Armance and his mother a complete withdrawal from society and thereby a kind of suicide.

Octave and Armance's fate is an ironic one within the Stendhalian universe, for in Stendhal's love ethic, first stated explicitly in *On Love* and implicit throughout his work, physical love is of but secondary importance to the noblest form of love possible – that is, passionate love, which does not necessarily imply consummation. Octave and Armance's failure, then, is not due to Octave's impotence or even to their mutual inarticulateness but rather to the impossibility of their ethic. Since their values cannot receive the approbation of anyone, each is left unsure whether the other shares his/her values and succumbs easily to the temptation to believe that the other does not.

Such mistrust of the other creates an atmosphere of dissimulation that permeates the novel. Octave's mother remarks in the first chapter that he harbors "a depth of dissimulation unbelievable for his age" (*A*, 19-20). Indeed, Octave makes everyone believe that he enjoys the company of his uncle, the commander, when, in fact, he abhors him. He also withholds his true thoughts from Madame de Bonnivet, leading her to believe that he is interested in her religious and philosophical gibberish. His attentiveness to the attractive Madame d'Aumale is likewise a dissimulation. More importantly, he disguises his true feelings to Armance, and she in turn dissimulates hers to his. In lying to the other, each believes he/she is being faithful to the code of honor. The lie becomes necessary in order to maintain the code. As Armance puts it, "This lie constitutes all my strength against him" (*A*, 33). The pleasure of a sustained human relationship is prevented because it is outside the confines of an ethic that, forcibly turned in on itself, must have recourse to deception.

The Political and Social Dimension

Armance's subtitle, "Scenes of a Parisian Salon in 1827," was chosen by Stendhal's publisher, but it is one that Stendhal, who had originally proposed "Or the Saint-Germain Quarter" and then "A Nineteenth-century Anecdote," readily accepted. In a letter to another publisher whom he had sought out, he had specifically stated, "I have sought in this novel to depict current mores, as they have been for the past two or three years" (*Corr.*, 2: 79). Specifying "the past two or three years" would account for the fact that most of the action seems to take place in 1825, the year of the Indemnification Law. The novel, then, clearly has a sociopolitical dimension, although Stendhal claims that his own political views do not enter into it. In the letter just quoted he assures the publisher that "no one will guess whether the author is conservative or liberal" (*Corr.*, 2: 79). In his Foreword Stendhal expressed the hope that readers would accord this author the same indulgence they had given the authors of a recent play: "They presented a mirror to the public; is it their fault if some ugly people passed in front of the mirror? To what party does a mirror belong?" (*A*, 5). Also in this Foreword Stendhal pretended that the novel's author was a woman and that his only role had been to correct the style, adding, "I am far from adopting certain political sentiments which seem entangled with the narration" (*A*, 3). This kind of proleptic defense was, of course, not unusual, neither for novels of the period nor for Stendhal himself, and readers then as now recognize it as a literary device. Victor Brombert has pointed out that the "constant awareness of a sociopolitical background is what makes this minor novel a milestone in the history of realism. *Armance*, preceding Balzac's first major novels by several years, rings a new note."[18]

One of the political issues discussed in the novel is the indemnification of émigrés. In the 1820s the French government was considering whether émigrés – those aristocrats who had fled France during the Revolution and whose properties had been partially or entirely confiscated – had a right to compensation from the government for their losses. This question touched on the very relationship between the Revolution and the Restoration, for it would determine the extent to which the Restoration would accept continuity with some changes effected by the Revolution. We know from what he wrote elsewhere that Stendhal was totally opposed to the indemnification of émigrés, but in this novel he never openly expresses that opinion. No character argues the case against indemnification, and only Octave wishes the law to be rejected, but for bizarre reasons: "First, because, being incomplete, it seems to me hardly just; secondly, because it will force me into marriage" (*A*, 15). While his first reason might be political, he never explains it, and it is in contradiction with his thoughts on the nobility expressed elsewhere.

The law awarding compensation to émigrés does, however, have an important function in the novel. Tying Octave's new wealth to this law places the characters in a historically defined world. Octave's drama would have been a different one had his wealth come from other sources. The return of a part of the aristocracy's wealth constitutes a crucial moment in the history of this class and makes it imperative that Octave, as the only child, marry. The fear that one of the oldest noble families of France might not perpetuate itself literally haunts Octave's father, who rejoices that the Indemnification Law will, by making Octave an acceptable party, give him grandchildren. As the aristocracy is gaining in power, Octave is being asked to place his personal life in the service of his class and to procreate – something he is convinced he cannot do. Octave is a hero unwilling or unable to fulfill his role of reproducing.

Obsessed with possession and perpetuation, these Restoration nobles clearly have no desire to participate in the major historical struggle of the 1820s – namely, the campaign for Greek independence against the Muslim Turks. Indeed, the attitude of the French nobility to this crisis is not without contradiction, since the most ancient of French noble families proudly trace their origin to the Crusades. Octave's father likes to repeat that he has "a *certified* genealogy dating back to the crusade of Louis the Young" (*A*, 11). Armance incurs the undying enmity of Commander de Soubirane by pointing out that it was the Russians rather than the Knights of Malta (with whom Octave's family has strong links) who were defeating the Turks. For Octave, this struggle is subordinate to his personal agenda. He tells his parents and Armance that he is leaving to participate in the Greek revolution, but this is a subterfuge to cover his suicide. Octave could well have committed suicide in another manner in another place. This dénouement, however, raises questions about this noble class, which originally had a military role but has clearly lost its crusading zeal. This issue, perhaps more than any other, reveals the nobility as a class without a function.

The nobility appears to be losing its religious coherence as well. While Chevalier de Bonnivet promotes Catholic piety among the servants, the neo-Protestantism making its way into certain portions of the upper classes is reflected in Madame de Bonnivet, a character who is clearly the object of Stendhal's satire. This paragon of the "new spirituality" is not above intrigue or even the use of spies to achieve her ends, which include converting young noblemen to *"the religious sentiment,"* an expression Stendhal places in italics to establish his ironic distance from it. Stendhal also uses italics for Madame de Bonnivet's stock vocabulary, *"conscience," "intimate sense,"* and *"rebellious being."* The latter designation she applies to Octave, says the narrator, with the joy of a doctor discovering a long-lost fatal illness. The narrator's reference to her belief in intermediate beings who hover a few feet above men's heads and magnetize their souls underscores the ridiculous side of a movement that had attracted a number of well-known upper-class women. Madame de Bonnivet's theories and jargon derive in part from Kant and in part from Benjamin Constant and Victor Cousin, both of whom were influenced by German thought. Stendhal had a profound aversion to anything remotely related to German metaphysics, and he did not consider its theological offshoots an improvement over Catholicism, which he disliked as well, but for different reasons. Paradoxically, Madame de Bonnivet, the proponent of new religious ideas, also participates in the popular craze for medieval architecture. In a sarcastic aside, the narrator mentions that "Madame de Bonnivet took delight in building Gothic towers in Poitou and in believing that she was reconstructing the twelfth century" (*A*, 247). Building Gothic towers and building new religions were, for Stendhal, equivalent illusions.

Politics and mores remain in the background in *Armance*, but their presence permits Octave to pass judgment on his times, particularly his own social class. He is not proud to be a noble and, at one time, wishes that he had been born the son of a cloth merchant. If he could do so without shocking his father, he would, he claims, forsake his title. He fantasizes changing his name and becoming a math teacher or a valet. His frequent desire to be incognito or of obscure birth reveals a desire to escape from his class. As both a judge of that class and a participant in its life and activities, he is quite aware that the nobility is a dying class. In a conversation with Armance, he says, "We are like the pagan priests at the moment when Christianity was poised to triumph. We still persecute, we have the police and the treasury behind us, but tomorrow, perhaps, we will be persecuted by public opinion" (*A*, 143). Armance, as lucid as he is on this score, replies, "I see something even more false in our position, yours and mine. We are part of this class only to share in its misfortunes" (*A,* 143). What is a graduate of the Polytechnical School who is a noble to do? Octave is unable to love, but he is also incapable of living out his life in his class. While the class codes that govern their behavior determine their intimate life, Octave and Armance, incapable as they may be in their personal relationship, remain capable of transforming their malaise into a critique of their class.

Chapter Three

The Red and the Black:
The Play of the Text

The Novel of Representation

Le Rouge et le Noir (*The Red and the Black*) has justly been called "one of the most boldly original masterworks of European fiction."[1] Indeed, since it precedes by a few years Balzac's masterpieces, it might be called the first great post-Revolutionary novel in France. In the three decades prior to the 1830 publication of *The Red and the Black*, serious novels in France tended to be either studies of individual character or historical narratives. The former focused almost exclusively on a character incapable of piercing through his own solitude and consumed by his own problems. While some of these narratives evinced social and societal concerns, the problems of the individual were generally not integrated into the complex realities of his time. In the latter, a society was evoked, but one that existed in the past. *The Red and the Black*'s subtitles – "Chronicle of the Nineteenth Century" on the title page and "Chronicle of 1830" at the beginning of book 1 – identify it as both contemporary and grounded in a societal complex. A number of markers in the novel (such as allusions to contemporary historical figures and events) further contribute to maintaining the plot within a contemporary frame. It is, therefore, a referential novel, a narrative that assumes some knowledge that is extratextually derived. The reality it refers to – namely, France under Charles X – would have been known to readers of 1830. It is in this society that Stendhal places a talented young man named Julien Sorel.

The novel begins with a representation of provincial life, specifically with a description of Verrières as one of the prettiest towns of Franche-Comté. The narrator notes its white houses and their peaked, red-tiled roofs, the vigorous chestnut tress, and the Doubs river that flows a few hundred feet below its fortifications. The second paragraph continues this line of description but introduces the first jarring element as the narrator depicts the industrialization of the region. He notes that the torrent that runs down from the mountain powers a large number of sawmills, thereby providing a certain well-being to most of the inhabitants. He points out that what has really enriched this small town is the manufacture of printed cloth, known as Mulhouse calico. By the following paragraph, when the narrator describes the nail factory, industry is seen as clashing with the beauty of the region. Immediately on entering the town "one is dizzied by the noise of a loud machine of terrifying appearance. Twenty heavy hammers, falling with a noise that makes the pavement shake, are lifted by a wheel powered by the water of the torrent. Each of these hammers produces each day I don't know how many thousands of nails" (*RB*, 1:6).

The contradiction between the beauty of the village and the deafening noise is but one of the contradictions Stendhal establishes. Industry takes a toll on the quality of human life, which the following lines make clear: "It's young, fresh, and pretty girls who prepare for the blows of these heavy hammers the small bits of iron which are rapidly transformed into nails. This work, which seems so rough, is one of those which astonish the traveller the most" (*RB*, 1:6). No direct judgment is passed here – the phrase referring to the young girls is almost in apposition – but the suggestion is clear: these young, fresh, and pretty girls are not meant to work in nail factories. The novel exhibits a picturesque code in the first paragraph, but already in the second and third paragraphs, this code, as Gérald Rannaud has pointed out, yields to an economic code that shatters the coherence of the first paragraph.[2] The new prosperity entails a process of dehumanization. Representation in Stendhal does not preclude narratorial judgment.

Stendhal's critique of provincial society extends to its moral conditions, particularly to the role played by petty concerns about money. Three-fourths of the inhabitants of the village, claims the narrator, are constantly talking in terms of "bringing in revenue." They are quite proud of the beauty of the area, "but it's because it attracts people from the outside whose money enriches the hotel keepers, something which, through the tax mechanism, *brings revenue to the town*" (*RB*, 1:14). Beauty has a monetary value as a tourist attrac-

tion. This attitude translates into a utilitarian view of nature. The
mayor sees no beauty in trees, only shade and lumber, and he is
wont to impose the hand of man on them, insisting that the trees on
the ironically named *Fidelity Promenade* be trimmed.

Provincial life is further governed by the power of public opinion, characterized by the narrator as "the most irritating *despotism*"
(*RB*, 1: 10), which makes living there virtually impossible for anyone
who has lived in Paris: "The tyranny of public opinion – and what an
opinion! – is as *stupid* in the little towns of France as in the United
States of America" (*RB*, 1: 10). Monsieur de Rênal initially employs
Julien to make an impression on public opinion, and Madame de
Rênal is forced to agree to his departure to appease that same opinion. More pernicious still is the politicization of the countryside,
making it impossible to live there free of politics. In the first chapter
of book 2 Falcoz relates how he had retired to the countryside in
order to live quietly but had been forced to leave because his refusal
to align himself with one of the political parties there had made his
life intolerable. In 1830 provincial life is mired in greed, social
standing, and politics.

The second milieu represented in this "Chronicle of 1830" is the
Church. Stendhal, whose critique has much in common with the
anti-Jesuit polemics of his time, focuses on the seminary, the
Church's institution for training its future leaders. He stresses the
secular motivation of the young seminarians who attend this institution. They were almost all sons of peasants, he informs us, and "they
preferred to earn their living by reciting a few Latin words than by
digging dirt" (*RB*, 1: 303). Here, as in Verrières, economics domi-
nates spirituality. Or, as Julien puts it, "My companions have a firm
vocation, that is, they see in the ecclesiastical state a long continuation of this happiness: eat well and be warmly dressed in winter"
(*RB*, 1: 314). In such an environment the practice of intelligence
becomes immoral. In the eyes of his fellow students, Julien was guilty
of "that enormous vice: he thought, he judged on his own instead of
blindly following authority" (*RB*, 1: 308). The moral ambiance insists
on external form over internal substance: "Julien didn't aspire above
all, as did some of the seminarians who served as models for others,
to perform at every instant some *significant* action. In the seminary,
there is a way of eating a hard boiled egg which reveals the progress
one has made in the spiritual life" (*RB*, 1: 310).

The seminary episode has an important function in forming Julien's experience of life and might accurately be described as "the intermediate period of his initiation."[3] It permits him to acquire culture (it is there that he read Cicero, Horace, and Virgil), but, more importantly, it places him in an environment sure to test his survival skills. Living in the mayor's household in Verrières had exposed Julien to provincial politics, to the existence of secret societies, and to the consequences of personal jealousies. The seminary, which has many features of a police state, represents an encounter with a considerably more hostile society. One of the chapters that relates life in the seminary is entitled "A First Experience of Life." Julien himself recognizes that he is finally in the world "as I will find it until I've played out my part, surrounded by real enemies" (*RB*, 1: 309). This supposedly other-worldly community is in reality a microcosm of the real world, and the time spent there will prepare him to better confront the Parisian world.

There are persons associated with the Church for whom Stendhal has a clear admiration (Chélan and Pirard are two examples in this novel), and he does make a distinction between truly religious persons on the one hand, and those who use religion for political ends on the other. In this regard he was particularly harsh toward an organization known as the Congregation. The historical Congregation, founded in 1801 as a pious and charitable organization, had no political agenda. At the time Stendhal was writing *The Red and the Black*, however, the word *Congregation* referred, in liberal circles, to a secret society dedicated to advancing far-right political views and the agenda of the Catholic Church. There was indeed such a clandestine organization, whose proper name, however, was the Knights of the Faith. The liberal opposition constantly denounced the real and imagined maneuvers of what it called "the Congregation." In his depiction of this association, Stendhal reflects the liberal discourse of the time.

The incidences of the Congregation's presence in the plot of *The Red and the Black* are numerous. In Verrières Abbé Maslon, an agent of the Congregation, displaces Abbé Chélan, considered too independent of the association's intrigues. Monsieur de Rênal, though a conservative mayor, appears to be under the Congregation's surveillance, for when he protests the rental of a municipally owned house at a reduced rate to a Congregation flunkey, he is called to the bishopric for a talk with the vicar general, Abbé Frilair, who heads the Congregation in the area. The Congregation is present even in the seminary where it persecutes Pirard and manipulates the examination results. Abbé Castanède, the Congregation's chief agent in the seminary, is also revealed to be in charge of the Congregation's police for the region. The story of Falcoz is proof that the powerful Congregation is everywhere. Its power may be coming to an end, however, for, when it is defied by Valenod, the very man whose career it has advanced, it is unable to have Julien acquitted, even though a lot of powerful and influential people want acquittal and previous judicial decisions mentioned in the novel have been decided through influence.

The high aristocracy constitutes a third milieu represented in the novel. This class, depicted as preoccupied with birth, lineage, and propriety, is stricken with fear of another revolution and has withdrawn from intellectual discourse. As a result the ambiance of its drawing rooms is just as restricted as that of the seminary:

> Provided that no one joked about God, nor about priests, nor about the king, nor about people in public office, nor about artists protected by the court, nor about anything that is established; provided that no one said anything positive about Béranger, nor about journalists of the opposition, nor about Voltaire, nor about Rousseau, nor about anything pertaining to free speech; provided especially that no one ever spoke about politics, anyone was free to discuss anything he pleased. (*RB*, 2: 43)

That is, provided that no ideas were discussed. The fatuity of this society is clear to the reader. On the following page the narrator calls this situation "moral asphyxiation." Julien even believes that the seminary was less boring. Mathilde, herself a member of this milieu, lucidly recognizes that if she weds the Marquis de Croisenois, she will be bored the rest of her life.

Three chapters (22, 23, 24 of book 2) concentrate on the politics of the aristocracy, specifically on a right-wing conspiracy to invite foreign intervention in French politics. This episode, known as "the secret note," echoes several similar plots that occurred in 1818, when the allied armies then occupying France were about to depart. In late 1829, when tensions between the king and the parliamentary opposition heightened, liberal newspapers published several articles on the possibility that right-wing elements might once again call for a foreign military intervention. It is improbable that in 1829-30 the Right contemplated such action, but Stendhal's fictionalization of such a plot expresses the opposition's fears.

While gripping, his narrative of this plot should have reassured those who feared the Right, however, for the characters involved are divided among themselves. The conspirators include the prime minister and a renegade general associated with the government and possibly spying on its behalf. Others, including a cardinal and two bishops, want to restore to the clergy its holdings and enroll the peasantry in the cause. An aristocratic party, to which the Marquis de la Mole belongs, seeks to form military units throughout the provinces. The conspirators, who mistrust each other, clearly lack realism, and the foreign representative to whom they send Julien appears to turn them down. The nobility may still be capable of plotting, but it is incapable of effective action.

If the narrator's depiction of the Right is not flattering, neither is his representation of the liberals. Although the narrator admits in the second chapter to being himself a liberal and at various points acknowledges heroes of liberalism such as Béranger, Lafayette, and Courier, the liberals represented in this novel are mainly wealthy industrialists (Gros, the mathematician, and Altamira, the revolutionary, are the exceptions). Monsieur de Rênal deplores the fact that, because industry is flourishing in his village, the liberals are becoming millionaires. Moreover, liberalism is constantly associated in this novel with what is base and dishonorable. When news of the impending arrival of a king in Verrières spreads, liberal ladies flock to Madame de Rênal's drawing room to plead for a place in the honor guard for their husbands. After the ceremonies "the liberals saw to it that they illuminated their houses a hundred times better than the royalists" (*RB*, 1: 190). At evening receptions at the home of the Marquis de la Mole, there regularly appears a Monsieur Sainclair, a well-known liberal who comes to flatter the nobles in hope of thereby gaining admission to the Academy. Finally, the liberal party's ambiguous ideology is revealed at the end of the novel, when it supports Monsieur de Rênal, the denigrator of liberalism, now transformed into a liberal. That Monsieur de Rênal, albeit a nobleman, is also an industrialist, does, of course, make the transfer easier.

Monsieur de Rênal's political conversion should alert us not to unduly schematize politics in *The Red and the Black*. That a well-know liberal (Appert), an aging Jansenist (Chélan), and a high nobleman (the Marquis de la Mole) find themselves allies is an indication that the political situation is much more complex than would first appear. That Altamira, a foreign liberal and revolutionary, can be received in ultraroyalist milieus is somewhat astonishing. This could be explained in part by the fact that he is one of them, noble and rich. But does that not announce that the aristocracy is fragmenting? That a plebeian Bonapartist such as Julien should become the agent of an ultraconservative conspiracy and would be the only one to risk his life in this affair is but another example of the disintegration of old political homogeneities. Julien is astonished at his own presence at the meeting of conspirators, asking himself, "How can they say such things in front of a plebeian?" (*RB*, 2: 272). Indeed, he would be in a good position to blackmail the Marquis de la Mole.

As Erich Auerbach pointed out more than four decades ago, "The contemporary political and social conditions are woven into the action [of this novel] in a manner more detailed and more real than had been exhibited in any earlier novel."[4] This is the first time that the hero of a European novel must take into account so diverse a society, that so many social, political, economic, and religious factors act on the hero whose destiny is clearly related to contemporary historical circumstances. According to Auerbach, it is in this work that we first recognize "a modern consciousness of reality" (Auerbach, 404). If we consider modern realism as that which represents characters within a total reality – that is, a political, social, and economic reality – then Stendhal can be said to be its founder.

Stendhal's brand of realism must be carefully distinguished, however, from that of Balzac, who seeks to describe in detail the milieu in which the action of his novels takes place. A case in point would be Balzac's description of Madame Vauquer's boardinghouse at the beginning of *Le Père Goriot* (*Old Goriot*) in which first the neighborhood, then the grounds around the house, then its facade, then the room on the first floor and its furniture are described even before the owner, Madame Vauquer, is introduced. Stendhal's approach differs considerably, as his presentation of the seminary where Julien will spend several months of his life shows. Neither the neighborhood nor the building is described; rather, we are told, "From afar, he saw the gilded metal cross on the door; he approached slowly; his legs seemed to give way beneath him. So that is the hell on earth from which I shall never be able to leave! Finally, he decided to ring" (*RB*, 2: 289). What Julien sees is the man who opens the door, and then

> they went up two flights of a wide staircase with a wooden baluster, whose warped steps leaned towards the opposing wall and seemed ready to fall. A small door on which had been mounted a large cemetery cross made of white wood painted black, was opened with difficulty, and the porter made him come into a dark, low-ceilinged room whose whitewashed walls were furnished with two large paintings darkened by time. (*RB*, 1: 290)

The reader sees only what Julien sees. Indeed, a number of events in the novel are seen either through Julien's eyes or occasionally through the eyes of another character. Reality, in Stendhal, is generally filtered through the individuality of the hero.

The Red and the Black is Stendhal's reading of the Restoration rather than a representation of the historical Restoration. Much of what he describes can be validated as historically true, but his interest lies not so much in representation as in interpretation and criticism. He reads the late Restoration as a society in flux in which the centers do not hold. The Church is mired in intrigues and losing its ability to manipulate events (it cannot save Julien from the gallows). The nobility is disunited, steeped in nostalgia, and out of touch with the times while succumbing to bourgeois temptations (the Marquis plays the stock market). The times belong to those willing to stoop to the basest maneuvers to reach their personal ambitions. In making of Valenod the only winner in the novel, Stendhal is signaling the advent of a crass bourgeois culture.

The Self-Reflective Novel

The Red and the Black's importance as a representational novel and its role in the formation of European realism are not inconsistent with its status as a self-reflective novel. To some degree all novels acknowledge the imaginary character of the story they tell. In this novel, however, Stendhal emerges as an author whose work unabashedly reflects its own fictionality, whose consciousness of being a novelist is evident even at the surface of his text and whose narrator enjoys highlighting the arbitrariness of his role. Moreover,

Stendhal adopts an overtly ludic – that is, playful – approach toward his novel. By attracting the reader's attention to his own playfulness, he is exercising his power as a writer to establish the modes according to which his novel may be read.

The playfulness begins with the title, *The Red and the Black*. For many years this title was interpreted as designating a choice of careers: the red represented the uniform of the soldier; the black, the cassock of the priest. This interpretation coheres with Julien's own belief that, in the previous generation, he would have become a soldier while, in his own times, he can have a future only as a priest. This reading is corroborated by a newspaper article appearing 10 days or so after Stendhal's death in 1842, in which the critic Paul-Emile Forgues affirms that Stendhal had late in life revealed to his friends who were perplexed about the title that "the Red signifies that, had he lived earlier, Julien would have been a soldier, but at the time during which he lived, he was forced to take on the cassock."[5] The textual support and this testimonial notwithstanding, this reading presents a number of problems.

First, what seems so obvious was not understood by Stendhal's contemporaries. "I don't know who is the red and who is the black," admitted Jules Janin in his review of the novel in 1830.[6] Twelve years after the book's publication readers were still asking themselves what the title could mean, according to Forgues. Perhaps this interpretation did not occur to Stendhal's contemporaries because the traditional and historical color of the French uniform is not red but white (under the ancien régime) or blue (under the republic and the empire). The dragoons who stimulated Julien's military ambitions in his childhood wore long white coats. In this period the soldiers who wore red were the British, whom Julien is certainly not dreaming of joining. Supporters of the traditional interpretation have replied that the sartorial reading of the title is but symbolic of a political interpretation: the antithesis between the military state and the ecclesiastical state, between the Empire and the Restoration. Others have pointed out, however, that during the Restoration, it is generally white rather than black which designates the far Right.

A number of other readings of varying degrees of plausibility have been proposed: the red flag of revolution versus the black of the Congregation; the red of passion versus the black of ambition – "black ambition," as the text puts it; the red of love versus the

black of death; or even, to salvage the military/clergy opposition, the
red of military valor versus clerical black.[7] These oppositional readings pose several problems, not the least of which is the author's
choice of the conjunctive *and* over the disjunctive *or*. If Stendhal
wanted to stress an opposition, whatever that opposition might be,
why would he not have chosen as his title *The Red* or *the Black*?[8]
The conjunction may very well signal the protagonist's inability to
choose between the options. Nonoppositional readings include red
and black as the colors of the robes of the judges who condemned
Julien, a reference to the red and black flag that momentarily flew
over the Tuilleries during the 1830 revolution, and red and black as
the colors of chance.

All these readings assume that the title is somehow related to
what goes on in the story, that it is a gloss on the meaning of the
story. If we do not limit ourselves to that assumption, however, we
might then suggest that the connotations of game and play represented within the title are directed at textuality itself. Why might not
red and black, the colors associated with many types of games, be a
signal that *the text itself* is a game? In a letter to his sister Pauline,
Stendhal had once expressed the wish that "one could situate life
where one wants, like a pawn on a checkerboard" (*Corr.*, 1: 482).
Might it be that he who wished to put life on a checkerboard, to put
life on red and black, has found the ability to do just that in the
novel? In his *Journal* Stendhal speaks of playing Red and Black (*J*,
1: 195), a nineteenth-century game of chance to which there are
references in other writers. In choosing Red and Black as the title of
his novel, might Stendhal not be signaling that this text is also a game
and inviting us as readers to play along?

These are questions only, and they might well remain at that
level were there not other indicators in *The Red and the Black* of a
ludic concept of textuality. The flagrant contradiction that strikes the
reader in opening the book is one such indicator. On the left, we
find a note from the editor – a fictitious editor, of course – which
announces that this novel was written in 1827. This note does not
appear in most of the English translations of the novel, but it is not
unimportant, for it contradicts the subtitle on the facing page, which
announces that this is a "Chronicle of 1830." A chronicle of 1830
written in 1827? And what are we to make of the footnote by the
same "editor" in the eighth chapter of book 2, in which he indicates

that the page in question was composed on 25 July 1830 and printed
on 4 August? Or the same editor's remark later still that the characters are "French people of 1830" (*RB*, 2: 258)? Or the cardinal who
analyzes the political situation "in 1830" (*RB*, 2: 270)? Or the allusions within the text to events that historically took place in 1830,
such as the performance of *Hernani*?

Even more striking are the epigraphs that are not drawn, as Ann
Jefferson has pointed out, from the authoritative texts of Stendhal's
culture.[9] The fact that most of them claim to cite contemporaries
(some of them undistinguished acquaintances of Stendhal) might
lead the reader to question the import the author attributes to them.
The skillful reader should also be alerted by the epigraph of the first
book, which has now become well-known: "The truth, the bitter
truth." These are given as the words of Danton, who is mentioned a
number of times in the novel proper and whose verbal presence has
a function in the text's thematic structure. What is frequently over-
looked is that there is no record of Danton ever having said or written these words (curiously, they are paraphrased in the novel by
Abbé Pirard). The lead epigraph to the novel, which seems to tell us
that we are going to be told the truth, the bitter truth, is a fabricated
quotation and therefore "false." If we turn to the first chapter, we
find another epigraph, in English:

> Put thousands together
> Less bad
> But the cage less gay

This enigmatic quotation is attributed to Hobbes. That attribution,
however, also appears to be false, since no such sentence can be
found in Hobbes's work. But lest we not catch the fact that this is a
false attribution, Stendhal disposes the quotation typographically on
the page as if it were a poem. Hobbes did not, of course, write
poetry. The epigraph to both the first book and the first chapter are
false. This should provide a very strong clue as to how we should
read the remaining epigraphs and perhaps how we should read the
novel.

The epigraph, much in fashion during the Restoration, had as its
function to summarize, illustrate, explain, and justify the meaning
that the author was giving to the chapter or book. It was intended as

an authoritative gloss on the text that would sanction the text through the prestige of a well-known author. The epigraph functions therefore as a metatext – that is, one whose function is to comment on still another text. The potential for textual play is already present within the nature and function, as traditionally defined, of the epigraph. But what happens when an author uses epigraphs that are imaginary, or misattributed, or misquoted, or simply unverifiable? Jean-Jacques Hamm has found that only 15 of the 73 epigraphs of the novel are actually by the author cited.[10] Is Stendhal, so famous for his penchant for "small true facts," not signaling to the reader – insisting even – that in a literary text we are dealing not so much with verifiability and referentiality as we are with textual play? Why else would he frequently have recourse to fabrications that, as was the case with the Hobbes attribution, call attention to their falsity?

Another epigraph of this type opens the second chapter of book 2. The longest epigraph of the novel, it relates the thoughts of a young man who feels intimidated and gauche in the first salon he has attended. He sounds a lot like Julien – or the young Henri Beyle. The attribution? Kant! Needless to say, this text can be found nowhere in Kant, and its substance and tone are so far removed from the ponderous Kantian text that the reader should be expected to detect the fabrication. Still another example of this type heads chapter 40 of book 2: "It's because I was then foolish that I am today wise. O philosopher who sees only the fleeting moment, how short-sighted is your vision. Your eye is not made to follow the subterranean work of the passions" (*RB*, 2: 425). The adjective "foolish," given as the masculine *fou* in French, would suggest a male author. The attribution? *Madame* Goethe! (Several English translations, as well as some French editions, have inappropriately corrected Stendhal and given "W. Goethe" as the source.) These and other glaring examples of such procedures lead us to conclude that the false attributions and even the misquotations are deliberate, that they are part of a signaling system whose function is to remind us that this is, after all, a game. While admitting that epigraphs also have as their function to comment on the text and to "augment the sensation, the emotion of the reader" (*J*, 5: 64), to quote Stendhal, and that some of them "play a tonal or prefigurative role,"[11] the epigraphs should be seen more as indicators of narrative situation, as clues to how we should read the text – namely, as a fictional game.

To further illustrate the ludic use of the epigraph, let us turn to the best known epigraph of all, and the one taken most seriously – namely, the epigraph of chapter 13 of the first book: "A novel is a mirror that one carries along a road" (*RB*, 1:133). The attribution is Saint-Réal. The quotation is an important one since it is paraphrased by the narrator in chapter 19 of the second book and is frequently used to argue for a realistic orientation in Stendhal. But let us look again at this epigraph. It is not, first of all, by Saint-Réal. Stendhal scholars have thoroughly searched the work of this seventeenth-century historian to find this quotation, but their search was in vain. This most famous of Stendhalian epigraphs is yet another false attribution. But there may be still another ludic dimension at work here. We need to recall, first, that Saint-Réal had published in 1672 a fictional work entitled *The Spanish Conspiracy against Venice*, which was long thought by its readers to be a work of history. Stendhal very much appreciated this book, "which is probably nothing but a novel" (*M*, 2:151), he says. Saint-Réal, then, is the author of a work whose fiction has been taken for a description of historical reality. Albert Sonnenfeldt has pointed out the possible pun on *réaliste*/Réal,[12] but the word *réaliste* as a literary category does not appear to have been in use in 1830. Yet, there may still be a pun and probably a bilingual one (readers of Stendhal's journal and correspondence know that bilingual punning was one of his favorite activities): Réal, r-e-a-l, giving the English *real*: Saint Réal: Saint-Real.[13] Are we not dealing with an ironic veneration of the real? Does the name Saint-Réal not function in the same way as the name of Mathilde's cousin, mentioned in the second book, Mademoiselle de Sainte-Hérédité? Perhaps Stendhal is suggesting that to worship the real is just as silly as to worship heredity. In literature, everything is verbal and nothing is real.

A recognition of the playfulness within the name Saint-Réal effects in turn our reading of the paraphrase of this epigraph in chapter 19 of the second book. The passage is well known: "Well, sir, a novel is a mirror which strolls along a highway. Sometimes it reflects the azure of the skies, at other times the mire in the gutter. And you will accuse the man who carries the mirror on his back of being immoral! His mirror shows the mire and you accuse the mirror!

Accuse instead the highway where the gutter is, or better still, the highway inspector who allows the water to stagnate and the gutter to form" (*RB*, 2: 224). Given the status of the epigraph from which this passage derives, can we continue to claim that Stendhal is in this instance engaging in a serious celebration of realism? Sonnenfeldt has already commented that "the figurative meaning of the mirror is rendered comical by a reduction to the literality of the highway inspector" (Sonnenfeldt, 109). If we replace this text within its context, we are faced with still more evidence that Stendhal is playing with the whole idea of referentiality.

The passage just quoted is part of three dozen lines of text enclosed within parentheses. This parenthetical digression is inserted immediately after the narrator has reported that Mathilde has spent half the night singing to herself an aria from that evening's opera: *"Devo punirmi, devo punirmi,/Se troppo amai."* This parenthesis is given as a commentary on Mathilde's behavior. "This page will harm the unfortunate author in several ways" (*RB*, 2: 223), it begins. He will be accused, he claims, of indecency for such a portrait of Mathilde. But, he protests firmly, "This character is completely imaginary, and even imagined outside the social habits which will assure so distinguished a rank to the civilization of the nineteenth century among all other centuries" (*RB*, 2: 223). No such young women exist, he goes on to elaborate. Then he slips in the seven or eight lines we have just quoted on the novel as mimesis only to conclude the parenthesis with the words, "Now that it is understood that Mathilde's character is impossible in our century" (*RB*, 2: 224).

We seem to be faced with two conflicting lines of defense: (a) Mathilde is a purely imaginary character who resembles in no way anyone existing in her own time; (b) this is a novel, and novels reflect reality, for which the author cannot be blamed. The first defense is usually read as ironic, as an oblique Stendhalian commentary on the prudence and calculation of young, aristocratic, Parisian women. And surely, it is that. The irony of the first defense does not, however, imply the truth of the second. The play involved in the epigraph, which this text incorporates in paraphrase, and the mockery of the veneration of the real that we detected in that epigraph have as their purpose to teach us how to read *this* text. Whatever role mimesis might play in Stendhal's concept of the novel, this novel is not a reflection of *la sainte réalité*. The second defense, though not ironic in the same sense as the first, is not to be taken at face value.

The title and the epigraphs, then, emerge as markers of textual play and as invitations to recognize the author's playfulness. Significantly, the novel's last four chapters, after Julien has been condemned to death, contain no epigraphs or chapter titles. Recognizing playfulness as one of the terms in which *The Red and the Black* produces itself as literary communication permits a number of fresh readings of some aspects of the novel. One of these is the famous presage at the beginning of the novel. Julien has stopped in the church on his way to the mayor's house and he notices on the kneeler "lying there as if it were intended to be read" (*RB*, 1:45) a piece of printed paper, presumably a newspaper, which reads, "Details of the execution and last moments of Louis Jenrel, executed at Besançon, on" (*RB*, 1:45). The paper is torn so that no other details are available, except the words "the first step" (*RB*, 1:45) on the reverse side. Julien remarks that the poor fellow's name ends like his own.

This incident has disturbed Stendhal critics, some of whom have dismissed it as an unfortunate influence of Walter Scott, while others have considered it too obvious or crude. But the device is neither as obvious nor crude as commentators have thought. Louis Jenrel is, of course, an anagram for Julien Sorel. Julien himself only recognizes part of the anagram – that is, that his name and that of the executed man end with the same syllable. The sophisticated reader, while damning Stendhal for so cheap a trick, congratulates himself for recognizing the full anagram. If we have taken up Stendhal's invitation to consider the text as play, however, we may recognize that Stendhal has not finished with the reader.

While thinking that he is smarter than Julien, the reader has himself recognized only one of two possible anagrams. The 11 letters that compose the name Louis Jenrel and the name Julien Sorel also compose the phrase *Je lis un rôle*: "I play a part." Armand Hoog, who first proposed this anagram,[14] points out, correctly, the numerous allusions in *The Red and the Black* to role-playing, acting, and theater. The narrator in fact mentions Julien's "role" 22 times. It is certainly possible to speak without exaggeration of "Beyle's constant theatrical viewpoint" (Hoog, 137). And, indeed, the anagram can be explained at the level of the psychology of character.

Julien, as we know, is forever playing a role: he is a hypocrite in the etymological sense, an actor onstage. A better explanation, however, could be found at the level of narration. Of course, Julien is playing a part, that part written by the author. "Who could have put that paper there?" (*RB*, 1: 45) asks Julien. The answer is, of course, Stendhal.

The Fieldingesque presence of the narrator within the text further contributes to the perception of the text as play. His oblique interventions – by which he criticizes his characters for being lyrical or unsophisticated when it is clear that he has admiration for such attitudes – invites readers to play along, to join in the game of guessing which of his interventions is ironic and which is not. When Julien weeps at Valenod's cruelty toward the poor in the workhouse, the narrator admits that he has "a poor opinion of him" (*RB*, 1: 242). Clearly we have a case of what Victor Brombert defined as Stendhal's way of affirming sensitivity while transferring its responsibility to the fictional character.[15] Were this always the case, the reader would only need to change the marker from negative to positive for each intervention and the decoding would become automatic and predictable. These narratorial interventions are, however, not all to be read obliquely. When Julien does not know what to answer when Madame de Rênal asks him, "Have you no name other than Julien?" (*RB*, 1: 144), because such a question had not been foreseen in his plan, the narrator comments on "the stupidity of making a plan" (*RB*, 1: 144). Clearly, the narrator is here passing a negative, albeit paternal, judgment on his character. For all Julien's plan-making, he cannot foresee all contingencies. Likewise, the reader can never foresee whether the narrator's commentary will need to be taken at face value or ironically – whether, in fact, he is criticizing Julien or adopting the language of Julien's critics.

One of the reasons for this unpredictability is that this text is telling the story of two Juliens. There is the Julien of *The Red and the Black*, whose story we all know well, and whom we might call the narrative Julien. But Stendhal is also telling us the story of another Julien, a hypothetical Julien, alternatively more sophisticated or less hypocritical, who would not make all the blunders the narrative Julien makes. This other Julien, whom we might call the narratable Julien because he always stands in a relationship of potency to narration, has a modal existence only – that is, he is presented only in the pluperfect subjunctive or sometimes in the past conditional. Ben-

jamin Bart has pointed out that there are approximately 150 occasions in *The Red and the Black* when Stendhal uses these tenses to
tell us "what would have happened if."[16] Bart has called these short
narratives, which run parallel to the narration proper, para-stories.

Among the many examples cited by Bart is one which occurs
during Julien's courtship of Maréchale de Fervaques. As he narrates
this story, Stendhal envisages differing possible developments of it.
What if Julien had been more hypocritical in his tactics? "If Julien
had had the idea of adding some phrases filled with German mysti-
cism, high religiosity, and Jesuitism, the Maréchale would immediately have considered him among those superior men who are called
to regenerate their times" (*RB*, 2: 306-7). If Julien had acted in this
way, then this is the way the story would have developed. But Julien,
of course, did not act in this way. Stendhal, incidentally, applies the
same procedure to Madame de Fervaques herself. Speaking precisely
about her, he writes, "How irritated would have been her pride if little Tanbeau, who had appointed himself to spy on Julien's activities,
had been able to inform her that her unopened letters were thrown
haphazardly in Julien's drawer" (*RB*, 2: 328). But, in fact, she was not
apprised of that.

Stendhal's procedure is somewhat akin to what is done in a
series of children's books, in which at various points in the plot the
reader is asked to choose from one of several possible outcomes.
Depending on the choice, the reader is directed to a specific page
where the story will continue as a consequence of the choice made.
At another point, another choice will be called for, with the same
procedure applying. This is a game, and these books are clearly mar-
keted as such. Stendhal cannot allow us to choose among several
possible outcomes, but he *can* tells us what would have happened if
indeed Julien had chosen to act in one way rather than another. The
same technique is also used with other characters, though less so.
Sometimes it is not the narrator who makes these kinds of conjec-
tures but the character.

One example occurs when Julien is in prison and thinking of
what could have been: "Colonel in the hussars, if we had had a war;
embassy secretary in peacetime; finally ambassador . . . because I
would have learned the profession quickly . . . and even if I had been
but a fool, does the son-in-law of the Marquis de la Mole have any
rival to fear? All my stupidities would have been forgiven, or rather

would have been considered meritorious" (*RB*, 2: 446). Here Julien is thinking of the continuation of the novel, of that very novel which he had declared "finished" but a few chapters earlier. He is thinking of what could have been had he wed Mathilde. But, of course, he did not wed Mathilde. These para-stories, which another critic, viewing the procedure more broadly, has called "speculative counter-stories,"[17] underscore the arbitrariness of narration, since both character and narrator admit that the story could have developed differently.

The features we have discussed have as one of their purposes to lay bare the play of fictionality. Like the Marquis de la Mole who, astonished at Julien's poor spelling, says to himself, "Could everything Abbé Pirard told me about his knowledge be just some story!" (*RB*, 2: 26), the reader must tell himself, "All of this is simply some story!" Julien is playing a part, and when he has finished his part, he can say with justification, "My novel is finished" (*RB*, 2: 376). But the narrator, who has played throughout with other potential plots, has other ideas. Julien's novel may be over, but the narrator's is not. "Who could have put that paper there" (*RB*, 1: 45), asks Julien, who is unaware that he is the object of a game. He takes himself as a writer of his own script, as an actor within his own script, and even, to use Peter Brooks's phrase, as "the stage manager of his own destiny."[18] Before going up to Mathilde's room, and fearing that he would be beaten or even assassinated, Julien sends, as insurance, a short document "arranged in the manner of a story" (*RB*, 2: 186) to his friend Fouqué. What is interesting about this gesture is that Julien was "like a dramatist, moved by his own story" (*RB*, 2: 186).

This is a concrete example of a moment when Julien believes himself to be the author of his own story. Stendhal, however, has reminded us throughout that he is the author of this novel. When Julien, having attained success, proclaims, "My novel is finished," Stendhal produces a reader of this narrative, Madame de Rênal, who in her letter to the Marquis de la Mole offers a critical reading of Julien's story. The reading she proposes – or, rather, which she transmits since her letter is written under the instructions of a confessor – points to the failure of the novel Julien thought he had brought to a successful completion. Her reading leads him to recognize the inauthenticity of his novel and, after the assassination attempt, to abandon it. When he abandons the novel, Mathilde attempts to delay its closure by elevating herself to the role of its heroine.[19]

Were we to judge by what is said about novels in *The Red and the Black*, we should conclude that novels exist to teach us the game. Had Julien and Madame de Rênal read novels, the narrator tells us, they would have known what role to play, what models to imitate. Mathilde, who has read novels, is quick to measure her passion for Julien with the passion she has encountered in fiction. Yet the narrator does not appear to take novels as serious texts; he scoffs at their style – "one could have said, in the language of novels" (*RB*, 1: 152) – and Julien scoffs at their structure – "It looks like this is going to be an epistolary novel" (*RB*, 2: 177). The book's publisher, who briefly appears as a character in the second book, refers to this novel as "frivolous writing" (*RB*, 2: 258), adopting the very language of detractors of the genre since Boileau-Despréaux. Stendhalian characters – and Julien and Mathilde are no exceptions – inevitably find that life is not like novels. Mathilde, for example, has experienced in her first amorous encounter with Julien "misery and shame . . . instead of those divine raptures which novels speak of" (*RB*, 2: 199).

The novel is presented in this novel as something false. Geneviève Mouillaud has concluded therefrom that *The Red and the Black*, because it wishes itself a mirror, is in fact an antinovel in relation to the novels of illusion against which it is reacting. All great innovative works of fiction, she points out, are critiques of the fiction that precedes them – critiques, specifically, of their verisimilitude.[20] If this is the case, however – if *The Red and the Black* is a novel conscious of its differences and thereby its modernity – it is also important to stress that in denouncing the illusionary character of previous novels, Stendhal's work remains fully conscious of its own illusionary character, conscious that the mimetic function operates within a ludic framework. In a footnote after the conclusion of the novel, Stendhal acknowledges that the town of Verrières is his own invention and that he has personally never been to Besançon. Stendhal's much-vaunted mirrors reflect first the novel's own fabrication, its illusionary devices and procedures. *The Red and the Black* is a mimetic text that wishes us to know that it is a game. "In truth, I'm beginning to believe this strange novel," Madame de Rênal says to Julien in his jail cell. "It only seems true," he replies (*RB*, 2: 457).

The Quest for Happiness

Stendhal's original title for this novel was *Julien*, and it is clear that Julien is intended to be at the center of the reader's attention. After the first few chapters, in which he is absent, the focus is almost exclusively on Julien and increasingly on his inner thoughts and sentiments, which are revealed to the reader through an extensive use of interior monologue. Although deeply sensitive (he is an avid reader of Rousseau), Julien appears in much of what he does as a combative, aggressive character (he is a great admirer of Napoleon). Frequently unsure of himself, timid to the point of tears on occasion, he places a high value on his own will and on the necessity of executing the decisions of his will that then become a matter of duty and honor. Carrying out what he has willed is never easy for him, and he must frequently issue challenges to himself, usually couched in military terms, in order to execute what he has willed to do. He constantly makes plans in advance to avoid having to react spontaneously to events and, in effect, defines himself before being. Julien mistrusts his own instincts and attempts to conform to a borrowed model, to copy the life of another. Through his reflection on the life and career of Napoleon, he has constructed in his imagination an ideal image of who he is and who he is to become. Lacking noble birth, Julien intends to achieve greatness by the force of his will.

His situation is very much complicated by his profound consciousness of class difference. The novel seems intent on highlighting the question of class by the importance it accords to the matter of Julien's birth. On numerous occasions Julien alludes to his lowly birth, and at one point refers to himself as "a kind of foundling" (*RB*, 1:62). There is more at play here, however, than the reworking of the foundling motif of the eighteenth-century novel. Throughout the novel various characters, including Abbé Pirard, allude to a mystery surrounding Julien's birth. When the Chevalier de Beauvoisis spreads the rumor that Julien is the natural son of a close friend of the Marquis de la Mole, this story suits the Marquis, who in turn creates another persona for Julien. In a game with strict rules drawn by the Marquis, Julien, when wearing a certain blue suit, is to be transformed into the younger son of a noble friend of the Marquis. In these instances the Marquis treats Julien as an equal. Mathilde, on the night of the ball at the Duke de Retz's, seeing Julien with Count

Altamira believes that he has the appearance of a disguised prince. She plays with this idea as she needles Monsieur de Caylus with the possibility that Julien might be the natural son of some country squire or perhaps even of a Spanish duke imprisoned in Besançon by Napoleon. The Marquis de la Mole adds to this game when, having decided to allow Mathilde to marry Julien and anxious to show that Julien is of appropriate birth, he gives him a new identity as the Chevalier de la Vernaye. Abbé Pirard reports to Julien the arrangements, which include a gift for "M. Sorel, a carpenter in Verrières, who took care of [Julien] during his childhood" (*RB*, 2:378), and the implicit recognition of his high birth by Abbé Frilair. Julien's reaction is a telling one: "Is it really possible, he said to himself, that I could be the natural son of some great nobleman who was exiled to our mountains by the terrifying Napoleon? At each moment, this idea seemed to him less improbable. . . . My hatred for my father would be a proof of it. . . . I would no longer be a monster!" (*RB*, 2:379).

Yet unlike fairly tales, in which a character assumed to be of low birth is revealed at the end of the story to be of high birth, this novel makes no such revelation. Its persistent playing with the question of Julien's birth serves to highlight the very question of class, setting the stage for Julien's hostility toward the upper classes. His contempt for those above him is evident early in the novel in such phrases as "That's how rich people are!" (*RB*, 1:99). His taking Madame de Rênal's hand when her husband is present is motivated in part by his desire to mock Monsieur de Rênal, "to whom fortune has given all the advantages he could wish for" (*RB*, 1:114). Indeed, Julien's relationship to Madame de Rênal, who is not at all class conscious, is colored and complicated by his consciousness of class difference. When Madame de Rênal says to him, with no repressive intent whatsoever, "Be prudent, I order you" (*RB*, 1:145), Julien's reaction is far from serene: "He deliberated for some time with himself as to whether he should be angry at this phrase, *I order you*. He was stupid enough to think: she could have said, *I order it* if it was about something related to the education of the children, but in responding to my love, this assumes equality. One cannot love without *equality*. . . . [H]e let his mind wander into making commonplaces about equality" (*RB*, 1:146-47). Julien certainly considers the conquest of Madame de Rênal, "raised in the enemy camp" (*RB*, 1:165), as a class conquest. While she is astonished at the happiness she derives from Julien's love, Julien, says the narrator, "was at quite a distance from such thoughts. His love was still ambition; his joy derived from the fact that he, a poor, miserable, and despised being, possessed such a noble and beautiful woman" (*RB*, 1: 159-60).

Julien's attitude toward Mathilde is, in this respect, quite similar, although Mathilde, unlike Madame de Rênal, is highly conscious of class. When Julien receives a letter from Mathilde in which she declares her love for him, his reactions is, "Finally, I, poor peasant that I am, I have a declaration of love from a noble lady" (*RB*, 2: 164). Julien's ecstasy is briefly interrupted by the thought that he would be seducing his employer's daughter, but he quickly reproaches himself for having pity on a family of high rank when he recalls that the Duke de Chaulnes calls him a servant and that the Marquis speculates on stocks using information learned at the royal court: "And I, who have been thrown to the lowest ranks by a cruel providence, I to whom she has given a noble heart and not even a thousand francs in income, that is, no bread, *precisely speaking, no bread*; I, refuse a pleasure which presents itself! . . . My god, I'm not that stupid; everyone for himself in this desert of selfishness which we call life" (*RB*, 2: 165-66). Significantly, the last words of this chapter are "He was a god" (*RB*, 2: 170).

The issue of class becomes more pronounced in Julien's speech toward the end of his trial for attempted murder:

> Gentlemen, I do not have the honor of belonging to your class; you see in me a peasant who has revolted against the lowliness of his condition.
>
> . . . My crime is atrocious, and it was *premeditated*. I therefore deserve death, gentlemen of the jury. But even if I were less guilty, I see men who, without considering what pity my youth might merit, will want to punish in me and discourage forever that class of young people who, born in an inferior class and oppressed by poverty, have the good fortune to obtain a good education and the audacity to mingle with what proud rich people call society.
>
> That is my crime, gentlemen, and it will be punished all the more severely because, in truth, I am not being judged by my peers. I don't see in the jury box a single peasant who has enriched himself, but only indignant bourgeois. (*RB*, 2: 440-41)

This is, to say the least, an inflammatory speech, but we must be careful not to overpoliticize it. The bourgeois jurors, including their chairman, Valenod, would not at all be shocked by the idea of upward mobility, although they might be presumed to look askance at so rapid a rise as Julien's. It is not the content of the speech as much as its adversarial tone that would have offended the jurors. What might be seen as a political provocation on Julien's part is first of all a reaction, the text is careful to note, to Valenod's "insolent stare" and to what he imagines Valenod might say to Madame de Rênal. Class *is* an issue in Julien's mind at this moment, but the "indignant bourgeois" he is primarily addressing – namely, Valenod – is a rival for Madame de Rênal's affections.

The composition of the jury Julien describes, however, is historically accurate, for in the 1830s only those who had a certain measure of wealth could serve. Likewise, Julien's death sentence corresponds to the jurisprudence of the time. Stendhal based the general plot of his novel on the story of Antoine Berthet, who in 1827 shot at Madame Michoud and was condemned to death for the crime. Like Madame de Rênal, Madame Michoud was wounded only, but she too belonged to the upper classes (though not to the authentic nobility). Another contemporary incident, known as the Lafargue Affair, likewise attracted Stendhal's attention. In this case the young man actually killed the woman – a commoner – and even sliced her throat for good measure. He was condemned to five years in jail, but his sentence was later commuted, and he was freed after serving two years. Stendhal must have been struck at the discrepancy in the sentences: death for wounding a noblewoman; two years in jail for killing a commoner.

In this speech Julien stresses his difference, and the text, to be sure, frequently refers to Julien as "different." That difference is not only social, however; it is also, as a number of critics have noted, moral and psychological.[21] Julien is a stranger, to be sure, but he would be so in any social class during this period: he was a stranger even within his father's home. The many references to Julien as the *son of the carpenter* must be understood in this context. This expression, which appears about 20 times in the novel and which Julien himself uses, cannot be gratuitous. Properly speaking, Julien is not the son of a carpenter but, rather, the son of a sawyer. Antoine Berthet, whose story provided Stendhal with the outline of *The Red and the Black*, was not the son of a carpenter but a blacksmith's son. The numerous references to the son of a carpenter seem to have as their purpose to evoke another son of a carpenter who was executed for having challenged the society of his time.

Aspects of Julien's personality as well as aspects of his activities do indeed relate him to Christ. The scene in which Julien is interrogated by the bishop of Besançon who is astonished at finding "a doctor among the pupils of [his] seminary" (*RB*, 1:355) recalls the story of the young Jesus astonishing the doctors in the temple with his knowledge. Julien hauling pieces of wood on his shoulders might recall Christ carrying the beams of his cross. One might note as well Julien's pity for the poor, his refusal to defend himself when he is accused, his condemnation on a Friday, his invitation to two other prisoners to share wine, and his burial in a grotto. Fouqué, much like Joseph of Arimathea, obtains his remains. In a general way, of course, Julien is dealing with Pharisees. That Julien, a conniving and hypocritical Don Juan who attempts to murder his former mistress during the most sacred moment of the Mass, should be represented, especially at the end of the book, with some traits related to Christ might lead us to read these allusions as a parody. But the end of the book, where most of the rapprochements with Christ occur, is the moment when Julien is no longer a conniving Don Juan, when he realizes that this way had been false.

It appears more likely that through these references Stendhal wanted to render his readers more sensitive to the destiny of a superior man confronted with a mediocre society. This would certainly cohere with Romantic thematics. In evoking Christ, Stendhal may also have wanted to draw attention to the fact that this society that calls itself Christian and that condemns Julien is, in fact, hardly Christian at all. When Monsieur de Rênal explains to his wife that, were it not for Julien's reputation as a Latinist, he would never have thought of bringing "the carpenter's son" in the midst of his children, the reader can be sure that Monsieur de Rênal would never have thought of bringing the other carpenter's son, Christ, among his children either.

Julien's speech, so crucial to the reading of the end of the novel, needs to be read, then, as the words of a character conscious of his difference. In this speech he claims to be "a peasant who has revolted against the lowliness of his condition" (*RB*, 2:441) and to have been born "in an inferior class and oppressed by poverty" (*RB*, 2:441). The claim is not new, for on entering the Rênal household he had referred to himself as a "poor peasant." The narrator refers to him several times as a peasant, and both Mathilde and the narrator call him a rebel plebeian. A close reading of the text, however, informs us that though he may be called a plebeian, he may not properly be called the son of a peasant. His father, though of peasant roots and sometimes referred to as a peasant, is the owner of a sawmill and is well-off financially. The narrator twice refers to him as "rich" (*RB*, 1:9, 29). If Julien is poor, it is not because his family is poor. Abbé Chélan, who knows Julien and his family well, writes in his letter to Abbé Pirard that Julien is "the son of a rich carpenter who gives him nothing" (*RB*, 1:294). Significantly, the peasants in the seminary do not recognize him as one of them and consider him a bourgeois. Both Abbé Pirard and Mathilde refer to him as a "little bourgeois" (*RB*, 2:14, 143). But peasant or not, the role of the poor commoner suits Julien: it is a role he likes to play, for it coheres to the Napoleonic mythology to which he adheres.

In his speech to the jury Julien does not attribute political motivations to himself. He committed the crime for personal reasons and he is not, in his final moments, attempting to give it a political significance after the fact in the manner of Hugo in Jean-Paul Sartre's *Dirty Hands*. His speech is, however, a commentary on Restoration jurisprudence in which class *does* play a role in the administration of justice. While Julien admits to his guilt and concedes that, juridically, he has earned the death penalty, he attributes political significance not to his crime but to the motivation of the jurors. He thus validates an image of himself as a "rebel plebeian."

The nature of Julien's revolt, then, should not be misunderstood. Despite his Bonapartist sentiments, his sympathy for the inmates of the workhouse, and his attraction to Altamira's revolutionary politics, he does not seek to overthrow the existing social order, nor even to redistribute power according to merit. When he does attain influence, he has the directorship of the workhouse awarded to his father and another post to Cholin, a local flunkey of the Congregation. At no time does he propose that the existing hierarchical order could or should be changed. He seeks not to overturn the system but to benefit from its privileges. In this sense, he succeeded rather well, rising from being a tutor to becoming the Chevalier de la Vernaye without much resistance from society.

Although Julien himself never defines his ambition with any precision, it encompasses a desire to surpass the rest of humanity. Taking the day off from his duties at the la Mole household, Julien ventures into the nearby mountains. Soon, the narrator tells us, Julien was standing on a cliff, "sure of being separated from all men. This physical position made him smile because it depicted the position he was burning to achieve in the moral sphere" (*RB*, 1: 111). His visit to Fouqué is important in understanding the scenario he is constructing about himself. Just before arriving at Fouqué's, Julien had been in the process of writing: "He came upon the idea of indulging himself in the pleasure of writing his thoughts, something which anywhere else was dangerous for him. A square stone served as his desk. His pen flew: he was aware of nothing surrounding him" (*RB*, 1: 126). His thoughts and sentiments are highly poetic; they turn around love, romance, passion, and the sunset. When he arrives at Fouqué's, he finds Fouqué writing as well, "doing his accounts" (*RB*, 1: 127). The contrast between these two acts of writing puts into sharp relief the differing ambitions of the two young friends.

Fouqué, forever generous toward Julien, offers him a partnership in his logging business. Although this would give Julien financial security, he refuses to accept, not even for the seven or eight years Fouqué proposes. Julien reasons that by the end of this venture into business, he would be 28 – the age by which Napoleon had accomplished his greatest deeds – and he worries that by that time he might have lost the sacred fire essential to the attainment of fame. Julien has refused the temptation of mediocrity. He had done so once before when he had the opportunity to marry Elisa, Madame de Rênal's maid, who had inherited a bit of money that would have permitted Julien to live modestly as a Latin teacher. And he will do so again when Prince Korasoff offers him the hand of his wealthy cousin.

Julien's ambition provides the context in which his hypocrisy, which seems to have repulsed the earliest critics of the novel, can be addressed. Julien acts in a clearly hypocritical manner on numerous occasions. On at least three occasions, the narrator relates Julien to Tartuffe, the supreme hypocrite of Molière's theater, and Julien himself quotes Tartuffe when confronted by the Marquis de la Mole about Mathilde's pregnancy. While Julien's concealment of his true thoughts and sentiments is essential to his entry into the Rênal and la Mole households and the seminary, it is also clear that Julien is not an accomplished hypocrite. Had he been a better dissimulator, he could have integrated himself more successfully in the life of the seminary – something he was unable to accomplish, not even knowing how to hide his disdain for his fellow students. The narrator reports that Julien "did not attend to details, and the cunning seminarians attend only to details. . . . *[H]e thought, he judged on his own* rather than follow blindly *authority* and example" (*RB*, 1: 308). As a result he is called Martin Luther by the other students. He was, says the narrator, "too different" (*RB*, 1: 325).

An accomplished hypocrite would, as one critic has reminded us, have known that above all he needed to appear like the others (Imbert, 555). At the moment in his story when Julien needed hypocrisy the most, he seems to be unable to sustain it. He himself recognizes that he could not muster sufficient hypocrisy to live at the Valenods. He knows that he would eventually betray himself and would be unable to repress the scorn the Valenods inspire in him. A Tartuffe, however, would not at all have feared moving in with the Valenods. Similarly, when Julien is in the la Mole household, the narrator notes that "hypocrisy, to be useful, must stay in hiding; and Julien . . . had half confided to Mlle de la Mole his admiration for Napoleon" (*RB*, 2: 133).

Julien's hypocrisy, imperfect as it may be, is essential, however, to his ambition. The narrator stresses this connection at the beginning of the novel when he relates how Julien, having been sent to the mayor's house by his father, hypocritically stopped by the church on his way. The narrator claims to understand that this act would surprise his readers and goes on to explain how Julien had first wanted a military career until he realized that the Church was now the powerful institution and would have to be the means through which he would succeed in the world. Because Julien is a nonbeliever, dissimulation becomes a requirement for his success. In this respect, he bears some resemblance to the emperor Julian, known as the Apostate, who, according to nineteenth-century historians, had hypocritically pretended to be a Christian until he was safely on the emperor's throne.

Still, Julien clearly dissimulates as well in areas unrelated to religion. Why so? The answer given in the novel is that the times are so mired in hypocrisy that, paradoxically, it takes hypocrisy to protect integrity. Superior people are no longer allowed to achieve according to their talents if they are unwilling to hide aspects of themselves that those in positions of power and influence consider unacceptable. To achieve something in Verrières, it is necessary to have the protection of the Congregation or to involve oneself in political schemes. It is through this process that Abbé Maslon replaces Abbé Chélan and that the intriguer Valenod ends up being the only winner in the novel. Within the Church it is the Frilairs and the Castanèdes who succeed, rarely people of integrity like Chélan and Pirard. The aristocracy is closed to outsiders, and even those of noble birth need to intrigue and spend countless boring evenings in aristocratic drawing rooms – or at least this is what Julien thinks. What, then, is a bright, ambitious young man to do? Because he refuses to take refuge in mediocrity, hypocrisy becomes his only protection, his only salvation. Conditions and circumstances, it could be maintained, made Julien a hypocrite, not character. Julien, who believes he deceives others without deceiving himself, would consider his hypocrisy qualitatively different from that of the likes of Valenod and Abbé Maslon.

In this context Julien's crime appears puzzling. How can Julien's commission of this crime, which would destroy his career forever, be explained? In the late nineteenth century, Emile Faguet, then a prominent critic, saw no explanation for it. In Faguet's reading of the novel Julien had previously always been in control; hence, his lack of control over himself in attempting to kill Madame de Rênal is inexplicable novelistically. Twentieth-century critics are not unanimous on the novelistic validity of the attempt on Madame de Rênal, and those who do accept it, like the characters in the novel, differ on their explanations of it. Julien is not clear on his motivations, implying first that he had acted because he had been "offended in an atrocious manner" (*RB*, 2:392), which would seem to reveal honor as his motivation. This would appear plausible, since he had previously placed honor above ambition, but later he proposes one or the other of two possible explanations: "After all, I wanted to kill her out of ambition or out of love for Mathilde" (*RB*, 2:445).

Stendhal seems to have deliberately eschewed providing a clear motivation to stress the complexity of such actions and to give the reader some freedom of interpretation. What is clear is that Julien is profoundly offended by Madame de Rênal's letter. That offense may come in part from the fact that Madame de Rênal accuses him of hypocrisy: "It's with the help of the most consummate hypocrisy and by the seduction of a weak and unfortunate woman that this man has sought to find a station in life and to make something of himself" (*RB*, 2:383). Such an accusation, based on partial truth, must surely have stung Julien, whose memories of his liaison with Madame de Rênal had remained precious. His passion for Mathilde had never prevented the few months during which he and Madame de Rênal loved each other from remaining the privileged period of his life. Madame de Rênal's letter not only ruins his career; by accusing him of hypocrisy, it destroys as well – and perhaps particularly – the memory of this special period by debasing the love they had felt for each other. To attempt the murder during the consecration, the most solemn moment of the Mass, is to attack the God who had taken Madame de Rênal away from him. Abbé Frilair, then, is closer to the truth than he thinks when, in an effort to torture Mathilde, he suggests that the priest celebrating Mass was Julien's rival for Madame de Rênal's affection.

Why, one may ask, would Madame de Rênal, even under the influence of a priest, have betrayed the only man she had ever loved? But is her letter truly a betrayal or, rather, an entreaty addressed to Julien? We can assume that Madame de Rênal would have been deeply hurt on learning Julien's plans. The letter the Marquis de la Mole has asked her to write about Julien could then be read as a reminder *to* Julien. In a sense she is successful, since the attempt on her life destroys forever Julien's love – not for her but for Mathilde. It might be suggested as well that Julien, in proposing to the Marquis de la Mole that he write to Madame de Rênal for a reference, was himself appealing for help, for he did not need to do this. The narrator had been careful to specify that, on Julien's departure from the Rênal household, Monsieur de Rênal gave him a "certificate of good conduct" in which "he had a hard time finding enough superlatives to exalt his conduct" (*RB*, 1:274). With such a recommendation in his possession, why would he suggest to the Marquis that he write to Madame de Rênal? Surely he would know that such a request would hurt her – unless, of course, it was that he was seeking to be stopped.

Julien's path of ascent has, after all, been based on false premises – something he will recognize only in prison. Throughout the novel he has been highly conscious of the presence of others whom he has instinctively feared and constantly tried to impress.

Prison, as an escape from others, can therefore become a privileged place. To Mathilde and Fouqué, who are trying to stimulate his hopes for a release, Julien says,

> Leave me my ideal life. Your petty worries, your details of daily life, more or less irritating to me, would drag me out of heaven. You die as you can; as for me, I want to think of death in my own way. What do I care about *other people*? My relations with *other people* will be cut off abruptly. Please, don't talk to me about those people. (*RB*, 2: 247)

Julien recognizes that others cannot know what he really is; only he can know that: "I alone know what I could have done. . . . For others, I am, at the most, but a MAYBE" (*RB*, 2: 449; Stendhal's capitalization).

Despite this lucidity, Julien is not completely freed from his preoccupation with the judgment of others and particularly from his fear of appearing as a coward. His consolation is that no one will be able to see his cowardice:

> A few clearsighted people . . . could have guessed my weakness . . . but no one *would have seen it*. And he felt himself delivered from part of his suffering. I'm a coward at this moment, he repeated to himself . . . , but no one will know." (*RB*, 2: 465)

Self-approval is clearly linked to public approval. When he is walking to his death on the scaffold, he is pleased that he has not lost his courage. As Elizabeth Brody Tennenbaum has remarked, the eye of others is "internalized by the Stendhalian conscience."[22] It is not surprising, then, that it is only in prison, when he is separated from others, that he finds moments of peace. That serenity is assisted by the fact that in the jail at Besançon he is placed in a cell on an upper floor. Altitude in this and other novels by Stendhal is associated with liberation from day-to-day concerns. Only when Julien is liberated from the contingencies of the present can he taste happiness. The prison emerges as a place of freedom, as it will in *The Charterhouse of Parma*.

Throughout the novel Julien has been as preoccupied with love as he has with ambition, from which it is not always kept distinct. In the end, however, Julien rejects Mathilde, that extraordinary woman, for Madame de Rênal. Both women are exceptional in different ways:

yet while the former lives in the past and fantasizes heroic roles for herself, the latter is consistently depicted as authentic and whole. This is a distinction Julien had glimpsed at various times but of which he becomes fully aware during his incarceration. In the face of all of Mathilde's activities and proposals,

> Julien . . . was tired of heroism. He would have been sensitive to a simple, naive, and almost timid tenderness, while on the contrary, Mathilde's haughty spirit constantly required a public and *other people*. In the midst of all her anguish, of all her fears for the life of her lover, whom she did not want to survive, she had a secret desire to astonish the public by the excess of her love and the sublimity of her projects. (*RB*, 2: 419)

Mathilde is continuing to do what she does best – playing a part – while Madame de Rênal never assumes the role of anyone but herself. Only rarely does she engage in role-playing, such as manipulating her husband after receiving the anonymous letter, and then she is fully conscious that she is playing a role.

The distinction between the inauthentic and the authentic personality reveals itself in the manner in which the two women love, which the narrator classifies as "love from the head" and "love from the heart." Mathilde has reasons for loving Julien: when these reasons no longer exist she will no longer love him. The narrator had already noted Mathilde's cerebral love: "Love from the head is wittier no doubt than real love, but it has but fleeting moments of enthusiasm; it knows itself too well; it constantly judges itself; far from putting off thought, it is built solely by thoughts" (*RB*, 2: 222-23). It is appropriate that, at the end of the novel, Mathilde should be left with Julien's head, but not his heart.

In the final analysis, Julien believes that Madame de Rênal's love is purer, for she "always found reasons to do what her heart dictated: this young woman of high society [i.e., Mathilde] only lets her heart be moved when she has proven to herself through good reasons that it must be moved" (*RB*, 2: 335). Julien also sees in Madame de Rênal a faithfulness of which Mathilde is incapable. He says to Mathilde, "In fifteen years, Madame de Rênal will adore my son, and you will have forgotten him" (*RB*, 2: 424). The cruelty of the remark need not be stressed, but it should be noted that Julien wishes his son to be raised quietly and serenely, something Mathilde would be incapable of doing.

Stendhal placed a great deal of importance on his depiction of the love motif and stressed this aspect in a sketch of an article intended for an Italian review about his own novel. He had long reflected on the psychology of love, and he is attentive to the nuances of its development. Yet love is intertwined in *The Red and the Black* with the manner of going about the quest for happiness. There emerge in this novel two ways of engaging in this pursuit. One is the way of volitional control: it emphasizes control by the self, through deception if need be, of external realities and situations as a way of securing the future. The other emphasizes letting go, abandoning concerns of power and fame, listening to one's feelings, and enjoying the quiet happiness of the moment. Each of the novel's heroines represents not only a different kind of love but also, as John Mitchell has remarked, a different approach to the quest for happiness.[23] Mathilde constantly seeks to control people and events and seeks to act according to her own self-definition. Madame de Rênal, on the other hand, is more likely to accept people as they are and events as they occur. She is prone to heed her impulses rather than her will.

Julien thinks he can achieve happiness by controlling his destiny and thus aligns himself, morally, with Mathilde. This means he must control the esteem of others – those very others whom he disdains. Before his incarceration, even in the absence of others, Julien uses the point of view of others in order to judge his behavior. There are a few fleeting moments, such as when he is dining at the Valenods', when he recognizes that this way is false. The joy that Julien experiences while in prison comes to him at those moments when he becomes fully aware of this falsehood, when he realizes that the way of acquiescence, represented by Madame de Rênal, constitutes real happiness, that indeed it was not being made the Chevalier de la Vernaye that conferred happiness but the private moments spent at Vergy. Rousseau has finally won out over Napoleon.

If the way of control is false, is the alternate way possible? It can be argued that the love of Madame de Rênal is impossible in the society in which they live. Letting go can bring Julien happiness only in the perspective of his approaching death. Living in the present is possible only because he is now prevented from controlling his future. The values discovered by Julien at the end of the novel cannot be lived in Verrières. Stendhal has already destroyed this private way to happiness in his representation of Falcoz and Saint-Giraud at the beginning of book 2. This option is but an illusion, for it can succeed only in very precise circumstances that cannot be generalized. In the end, Stendhal sabotages the very option that Julien, after many trials, has chosen.

Chapter Four

Lucien Leuwen: Love, Politics, and Emancipation

A Character in Search of Himself

Jean Prévost suggested some years ago that in *Lucien Leuwen* (written in 1834-35) Stendhal seems to have invented the character first and the plot afterwards.[1] Prévost was thereby underscoring the experience of many readers of the novel who sense that its author has no very precise ideas on how to arrive at a conclusion – nor, for that matter, what the conclusion should be. We do know from Stendhal's notes that he originally had a conclusion in mind but that he abandoned it along the way. If, as some critics have suggested, one of the tasks of all plots is to forestall closure, then Stendhal has achieved at least that objective in this novel. Since the plot does not seem to point to a clear closure, it is the character of Lucien who becomes the center of interest.

The son of a wealthy banker, Lucien takes a commission as a second lieutenant in the army in order to prove himself. Posted to Nancy in eastern France, he pretends to harbor conservative views to gain access to aristocratic salons. In the process he falls deeply in love with a young widow, Madame de Chasteller, who resists him despite her love for him. Still, his affection for Madame de Chasteller alarms some of the young nobles who, using an implausible stratagem, convince him that Madame de Chasteller not only does not love him but is sexually active with other men. He thereupon returns to Paris where, through his father's influence, he becomes the top aide to the minister of the interior. In this position he is involved in a number of morally dubious assignments in which he acquits himself honorably. When it becomes clear to Lucien, however, that his father is attempting to manage not only his career but his love life as well, he finally rebels and moves out of the parental

home. His father then dies, and the novel ends as Lucien leaves
France to serve as embassy secretary in Rome.

Initially presented as a somewhat nonchalant young man with a
penchant for handsome uniforms, Lucien is beset with a fundamental
problem: he does not know what he is or what he is capable of.
"What am I, then?" (*LL*, 1: 106) is a question that does not cease to
haunt him. His reply to Madame de Chasteller when she remarks that
he is a strange man is quite sincere: "Truthfully, I don't know what I
am, and I would pay dearly anyone who could tell me" (*LL*, 3: 7). As
the son of a wealthy man, he has never had to *do* anything that
would show who or what he is. His disinterest in amassing a fortune
makes of him a decided oddity in a society depicted as preoccupied
with this subject. But if he knows that he is not interested in learning
his father's business and making money (an easy position for him,
who has all he wants in any case), he does not know what he does
want or even who he is. He is, throughout much of the novel, a
character in search of an essence.

Michel Crouzet has correctly labeled this narrative as a "novel of
appearances,"[2] for the society in which Lucien lives is replete with
persons playing roles. Not knowing his essence, Lucien, too, finds
himself assuming identities and pretending to be something he is
not. Early in the novel Lucien's cousin, urging him on to social success, counsels him to be serious and to adopt a solemn role. Lucien
answers that he fears that in less than one week "the *solemn role*
would become a reality" (*LL*, 1: 15). He is at least aware that a mask
after some time may stick to the skin, that the person wearing it may
never be able to divest himself of the persona he has adopted (this
did happen to the main character of Musset's play, *Lorenzaccio*,
published while Stendhal was working on this manuscript). The
mask had been important to both Octave and Julien in Stendhal's
two previous novels, but its role seems magnified in a society such as
the one depicted here, in which public opinion plays so dominant a
role.

Lucien does accept to wear masks that transform his speech,
beliefs, and appearance to suit the role he has chosen. In Nancy he
wears the mask of the right-minded person in order to be welcomed
into aristocratic society in general and Madame de Chasteller's society in particular. Dissimulation, he learns from this experience,
works. Such symbolic gestures as attending church services or

adopting a particular style of language make him acceptable to the local high society. Similarly, in Paris he effectively dons the mask of the *juste milieu* as he undertakes difficult missions for the government, such as managing the Kortis Affair and the election campaign, both assignments in which he musters his energies and talents for causes in which he does not believe. Paradoxically, the roles he plays are part of the process of self-discovery. The adventures he undergoes during the course of the novel contribute to answering his question, "Who am I?"

Lucien vests a great deal in what others (or at least certain others: his father, his mother, Develroy, Madame de Chasteller, Coffe) think of him, and it is not surprising that his problem is first imposed on him by others. His experiences, however, are meant to teach him that the labels others place on him are not at all reliable. He was expelled from the Polytechnical School because he was suspected of republicanism. But the reader knows that Lucien is no republican, even if he does have occasional republican sympathies. Nor is he, as some believe, a Saint-Simonian – a designation then sometimes associated with republicanism – nor a Jacobin as the king seems to think, nor conceited and self-satisfied as still others think, nor a government spy, as a churchman in Nancy proposes. The problem, then, has been wrongly put to him by his cousin Develroy. When the latter says to him in the second chapter that he is but a child who does not count for anything, someone who has only gone to the trouble of being born, he is, of course, telling him the truth: that a young man as rich as Lucien owes everything to his father. According to Develroy, Lucien should examine himself and see if he is worth anything. This is good advice, but Develroy, the incorrigible social climber, mitigates the value of his counsel by relating it to what others will think of Lucien.

While realizing that he must find some way to gain self-esteem, Lucien does not conceive of this self-esteem outside the opinion of his parents and Develroy. Throughout the novel he accepts responsibilities distasteful to him, such as his political work, solely because he thinks this will please his parents or his cousin. When Gauthier, his republican interlocutor in Nancy, asks him, "What do you care about other people's opinions?" (*LL*, 1: 119), Lucien responds that he has a vanity that he, Gauthier, could not possibly understand. When the novel is nearly complete, and Lucien still asks his father what opinion he should have of himself, he has not yet freed himself from this fundamental error.

Love and Blindness

While he is in the process of trying to determine what kind of person he is, or at least to prove to his father that he can at least be someone, Lucien falls in love. He is led to this state by a fall from his horse in view of a beautiful young widow who is watching him from her window. Ironically, Lucien, who has been told repeatedly by his cousin that he is incapable of anything, was capable – or so he thought – of one thing: riding a horse. The fall only renders more acute the need to prove himself, for there is now one more person to convince – namely, the woman at the window. This process will lead to his falling in love with this very woman. It is clear that this experience retards Lucien's discovery of an identity. Instead of convincing him that he is capable of something, his love for Madame de Chasteller affirms the contrary – namely, that he will never be able to succeed at anything.

In the initial stages and for some time thereafter, he contents himself with gazing at Madame de Chasteller's window from afar, unaware that behind the blinds she is also looking at him. When he first meets her, he finds himself paralyzed and unable to say anything. Then, when he is placed next to her at a dinner, the narrator tells us that he spoke little and that what he did say was insignificant. Readers familiar with Stendhal know that passion frequently impedes social grace and wit, but Lucien is convinced that he is but an idiot. He constantly discredits his talents and character, to the extent that these comments become a kind of litany. But is he really an idiot?

Lucien is in many ways blind. He does not see that certain things, inoffensive in and of themselves – such as the choice of an apartment or the amount of money that he spends – can harm him. "He didn't see," the narrator tells us, "with enough clarity" (*LL*, 1: 112) the effect of such actions on his fellow junior officers. "Lucien saw none of these things" (*LL*, 1: 115), the narrator adds shortly afterwards. Nor does he see potential friends and supporters: "He was blind" (*LL*, 1: 133). Moreover, he does not recognize that he is succeeding rather well with Madame de Chasteller. The narrator makes this clear relatively early in the novel when Lucien leaves an evening reception with a disquiet heart: "He was far from noticing the full extent of his victory" (*LL*, 2: 242). Other examples of this type could be adduced to show that Lucien is unable to see the world as it is.

This aspect of his character comes to the fore in the episode of the false birth. In order to get Lucien to leave Nancy and thereby Madame de Chasteller, Dr. Du Poirier stages a scene that makes the unsuspecting Lucien believe that Madame de Chasteller has just given birth. On the face of it, this scenario should not have succeeded: the baby is too old and the insinuations by the maids that Madame de Chasteller has had many lovers do not at all concur with what Lucien knows about the woman. Dr. Du Poirier was clearly taking enormous risks in mounting such a farce. Had he, an agent of Charles X, been discovered as masterminding such a plot, the legitimist cause would have been jeopardized. Moreover, since the beginning Du Poirier has been depicted as a deeply fearful man. How could he then undertake such a risky operation? He could do so only because, as an astute judge of men, he knew he could count on Lucien's blindness. Indeed, Dr. Du Poirier's crude strategy confirms that blindness.

The segment is, to be sure, one of the least plausible, on realist grounds, in Stendhal's fiction. Yet it is not the episode's verisimilitude that is important but rather its function within what Victor Brombert has called the novel's "poetry of unawareness" (Brombert, 104). Many of the novel's characters are blind to the reality around them, but Lucien and Madame de Chasteller's refusal ever to ask for explanations only compounds their problem. In matters of love, they prefer to envisage every explanation possible (except the correct one) than to ask an indiscreet question. It has never occurred to Lucien to ask Madame de Chasteller about Lieutenant Colonel Busant de Sicile, whom he wrongly believes to have been her lover. Lucien, who knows that most of the labels attached to him are false, is inclined to accept as true what is said about the woman he loves rather than question her about it. This refusal to ask indiscreet questions is a malady that afflicts, to some degree, all of Stendhal's heroes and heroines.

Lucien's problem is further complicated by the character of the woman he loves. Although the information given about her is

sketchy, Madame de Chasteller is repeatedly referred to for about
150 pages, until she appears quite suddenly. In several successive
occasions, when Lucien is not expecting her, she again suddenly
appears. She clearly terrifies him, and he occasionally thinks of her
as "the God that I adore" (*LL*, 3:7). No clear answer, however, is
provided to the major question about her: Why does she resist
Lucien's love? Since she loves him, there would seem to be no reason for a refusal. As her friend Madame de Constantin puts it,
"Where's the harm, good Lord! in a young widow of twenty-four,
whose only support is a seventy-year-old father, . . . seeking to
choose a husband?" (*LL*, 3:167-68). Madame de Chasteller does
object that her family would never agree to her marrying Lucien
since he is from the opposing party and not of noble birth. A few
pages later, the narrator confirms this impediment: "Almost every
day, her father made a scene about this subject. 'What! my daughter,
spending two hours every day with a man of that party and what's
worse whose birth does not permit him to aspire to your hand' " (*LL*,
3:86).

Is her refusal, then, based on social and political incompatibili-
ties? This explanation comes rather late in this long episode, and she
is not reported to have thought of it previously. The political
impediment is, to be sure, a serious one, given Madame de
Chasteller's family situation, but it would not have been a total
obstacle. While marriages between members of the aristocracy and
those of the wealthy classes were not the norm in 1835, they did
occur. In any case, readers know that Lucien and Madame de
Chasteller have put aside their politics in favor of their relationship.
Indeed, the political impediment, while important, does not appear
to be the only reason for a refusal of love. At an evening reception,
when she and Lucien have their first real conversation, Lucien
alludes to a suspicion he has. Madame de Chasteller asks whether
this suspicion could be somehow related to her. When he responds
in the affirmative, she is deeply troubled, although this feeling is
accompanied by the thought that Lucien is in love with her. Later
that evening the narrator tells us that she was in despair, convinced
that her conduct had been atrocious: "I have compromised myself in
front of all these ladies, and at this moment, I am the subject of the
most offensive and humiliating remarks. I've been acting for I don't
know how long as if no one was looking at me, at me or M. Leuwen.

This public won't allow me anything. . . . And M. Leuwen?" This name, pronounced mentally, makes her shiver: *"And I have compromised myself in M. Leuwen's eyes!"* (*LL*, 1: 296).

As in *Armance*, the question of the esteem of the loved one in the eyes of the lover becomes crucial. This is confirmed a few pages later when Madame de Chasteller, still in despair at the thought of having lacked reserve in front of Lucien, comes on the idea of entering a convent and remaining there forever – a solution also considered by Armance: "The only objection against this project was that everyone would be talking about her, speculating on her reasons, supposing some secret motives, etc. 'What do I care! I'll never see them again. . . . Yes, but I'd know that they are talking about me, and spitefully so, and that will drive me crazy' " (*LL*, 2: 237). Her personal honor and esteem, then, depend on the consideration of others.

Still more important is the opinion that Lucien might have of her:

> *"I've compromised myself in M. Leuwen's eyes,"* she repeated to herself in an almost convulsive manner. . . . "There was one fatal moment when in front of this young man I forgot that holy discretion without which my sex can aspire neither to the respect of the world nor to its own esteem. . . . I have forfeited forever, I've destroyed in one single moment of forgetting, the purity of the thoughts which he could have had about me. Alas! my excuse is that it's the first moment of disordered passion I've had in my life. But is this an excuse that can be said aloud? Can it even be imagined? Yes, I've forgotten all the laws of modesty!" (*LL*, 3: 238)

Similar thoughts assail her just a few pages later as she ruminates on her violation of that feminine reserve "without which a woman cannot be esteemed by a man worthy, in return, of some esteem. Faced with this accusation, her pain seemed to give her moments of relief. She got to the point of saying out loud and in a voice half choking with tears: *'If he didn't hold me in contempt, I would hold him in contempt'* " (*LL*, 2: 247).

These sentiments resemble those of Armance, for whom what is most essential is not to lose the esteem of the person loved. Indeed, if the other does not lose esteem for a person who so deserves, then that very person should lose esteem for him. This *morale du grand siècle* coheres with a natural bashfulness and an acquired prudery in Madame de Chasteller. To protect herself she welcomes impediments and creates some of her own. She wants to be loved by Lucien, but when she has a fleeting thought to take his hand and bring it to her lips, "this idea horrified her" (*LL*, 3:60). In her extreme reactions she bears still another resemblance to Armance. As with Armance, her hesitancy has no religious motivations (unlike Madame de Rênal). Madame de Chasteller does come to accept her love and does finally allow Lucien to visit her frequently and to engage in intimate conversations. What she does not do is reveal her love to Lucien in a way that is clear to him.

No reader can fail to note that the word *chaste* is embedded in the heroine's name. In French a phonological metathesis (Chasteller = *l'air chaste*) produces an even more striking resonance. One of the meanings of *l'air chaste* could be "seems chaste" or "pretends to be chaste," but that does not seem to be the meaning here. At one point Lucien takes note of her "candid and chaste physiognomy" (*LL*, 1:248) and later decides that, compared to the other women in her entourage, she has "the air of a goddess of chastity" (*LL*, 3:74). The French words *l'air de la chasteté* contain the metathesized phonemes of her name. What these two reflections of Lucien suggest is that Madame de Chasteller projects a chaste appearance and demeanor. Lucien's failure to be convinced by that projection is, ultimately, what leads him to fall into Du Poirier's trap, for he is curiously obsessed with the idea that Madame de Chasteller had had a previous lover, and he cannot cope with her being anything but a pure woman. In one of his monologues we hear him imagining himself telling her, "If your soul had been purer, I would have attached myself to you for life" (*LL*, 2:259).

Madame de Chasteller plays an important role in Lucien's search for an understanding of his abilities. The quality of his love for her is such that she functions as a standard by which he judges the political world of Paris and the frivolous love of Madame Grandet. After his difficult electoral mission, what seems to concern him the most is how Madame de Chasteller would assess his behavior. She has a moral weight that influences his vision of other persons and situations. Much like a lady in courtly literature, she is the ultimate judge of his actions.

The Novel of Politics

Lucien Leuwen, which has been called "the most searching political novel of the first half of the nineteenth century" (Hemmings, 154), might be considered a political continuation of *The Red and the Black* since it deals with the July Monarchy, the constitutional regime that succeeded the Restoration that had provided the political context of the earlier novel. The July Monarchy rose out of the revolution of 1830 and, after initially giving hope to liberals, dashed these hopes as it became increasingly conservative. That Stendhal wished to depict this regime is clear from the novel's second preface, in which he repeats his mimetic formula that "a novel must be a mirror" (*LL*, 1:5). This novel's political dimensions are already evident in its first sentence, where it is related that Lucien was expelled from the Polytechnical School for having participated in antigovernment demonstrations. Indeed, the polytechnical students, many of whom had republican sympathies, frequently appeared at antigovernment rallies, resulting in suspensions or expulsions for a number of them.

One of the novel's political messages is that the July Monarchy has betrayed the revolution that gave it birth. The nobility has been replaced by the upper bourgeoisie, which has arrogated to itself the power and influence formerly exercised by the nobility. The power that Lucien's father, Monsieur Leuwen, exercises is sufficient proof of that. It is the minister who must wait for Monsieur Leuwen and not the contrary, and the minister, Monsieur de Vaize, is perfectly aware of this when he remarks that a decree from the king can make a minister but a decree cannot make a man like Monsieur Leuwen. Toward the end of the novel we see the king personally ask Monsieur Leuwen to give him the votes he needs in order to get a law adopted. Monsieur Leuwen, like the high aristocrats of the ancien régime, lets ministers wait and lets himself be beseeched by the king. He recognizes that his power derives from the money he has amassed in his commercial dealings: "Since July, banking interests run the State. The bourgeoisie has replaced the Faubourg Saint-Germain, and banking is the nobility of the bourgeois class" (*LL*, 4:272). The revolution has therefore been betrayed, for power and privilege are still in the hands of a small, privileged group.

It has also been betrayed in the manner in which the July Monarchy has used the army for political and social repression within France itself. The text makes a number of allusions to "Transnonain Street," the location of an event that took place in April 1834 in Paris. An insurrection in Lyon earlier that month had led to demonstrations in Paris that were countered by such repressive measures as the massacre of Transnonain Street, an event immortalized by a now-famous Honoré Daumier engraving. The novel relates none of the circumstances of this massacre, but the reader is assumed to be aware of them. The recurring allusions to this event constitute a haunting reproach to a government born of liberal enthusiasm.

Indeed, Stendhal's novel highlights the new role assigned to the military. The first part of the novel contains numerous allusions to the use of the army to prevent workers from organizing. As early as chapter 2, before receiving his military assignment, Lucien anticipates that he will be involved in a war of cabbages against dirty, starving workers – and later he does participate in such a campaign. The narrator uses the occasion to describe the poverty, decay, and dirt in which the workers must live. "There was everywhere," he writes, "a sharp image of poverty which seized the heart, but not the hearts of those who hoped to earn a military cross by thrusting their sabers in this poor little town" (*LL*, 3: 323). In this particular campaign against the workers, the army ends up playing a ridiculous role. "Such was Leuwen's first campaign" (*LL*, 3: 20), remarks the narrator ironically. The army that three decades earlier had been the master of Europe is now reduced to waging war against "chamber pots and cooked potatoes" (*LL*, 3: 73).

In this government ministers and high functionaries do not at all surpass their predecessors, except perhaps by their corruption, hypocrisy, and professional jealousies. When Monsieur Leuwen proposes to Lucien that he join the minister's staff, his advice to his son is "leave your moral sense at the door when you enter the ministry" (*LL*, 3: 155). Political success, his father seems to be saying here and elsewhere, requires a large dose of cynicism on the part of the political aspirant. Indeed, this government appears to be engaged in all sorts of devious political schemes. It promotes a program designed to inhibit fraternity between the military and the working class as a way of conserving the military's effectiveness, should it need to be used against the people. Agents of the government deliberately provoke quarrels between workers and the army in order to maintain a climate of hostility.

Lucien becomes involved in this policy when he is called to manage the Kortis Affair. This fictional event, which had its counterpart in the history of the period, involves a provocateur on government payroll who had attacked a soldier and had been mortally wounded by the recruit. Lucien's assignment is to deter the agent from talking as he lies dying in the hospital and to prevent the police agency that had employed him from silencing him through poison. This incident proves to Lucien his ability to manage an extremely sensitive situation and to do it without losing his own honor, while it also gives him an insight into the sleazy side of government. More importantly, perhaps, it contributes to the picture of an administration hardened to its own crimes and concerned only with its own perpetuation. This viewpoint is reinforced by Lucien's assignment to assist the government in winning the elections in two key constituencies. Although Lucien again acts with energy, intelligence, efficiency, and, to his own mind, honor, the depiction of these events reveals an amoral cynicism on the part of a government willing to resort to whatever kind of manipulation is required to win.

In addition to being corrupt politically, the members of the government use their positions to enrich themselves personally. The minister of the interior, Monsieur de Vaize, plays the stock market using the inside information he receives through the government's telegraph system. Even the king engages in this kind of insider trading. The broker for many of these deals is none other than Monsieur Leuwen. This tendency of high-ranking officials to profit personally from their positions had been denounced by Paul-Louis Courrier, the famous liberal pamphleteer of the period. Stendhal gives voice to the same accusations as he depicts Louis-Philippe and his *juste-milieu* team as dangerous rascals.

If those who make up the *juste milieu* government are corrupt, there are no attractive alternatives in this novel. The legitimists – that is, those who still hold to the ideals of the Bourbon monarchy – are divided among themselves and described as pitiful, morally degenerate creatures who live in the past. Their society in Nancy resembles a theatrical production as its members engage in continuous role-playing. Lucien recognizes that "with them, everything, even laughter, is an affectation" (*LL,* 1: 217). Significantly, one of the

leading representatives of Charles X is Madame de Chasteller's
father, Marquis de Pontlevé. He lives on rue de la Pompe, a street
whose name evokes the empty ceremony to which the legitimists are
attached. His name, which in French evokes a drawbridge (*pont
levis*) or a drawn bridge (*pont levé*), suggests that he and his group
have indeed raised their drawbridges in order to cut themselves off
completely from contemporary nineteenth-century life. Ironically, in
Nancy this same group is given to following the advice of an
intriguing bourgeois, Dr. Du Poirier. While they have enough political power and organization to interrupt and monitor mail through
the local postmistress, their return to national power is not envisaged by this text.

The return of the Bourbons would not have been, however, the
only option as a replacement of the *juste milieu*, for in Europe in
1834-35 – the time the novel was written – republican ideals were
very much alive. Lucien has a natural sympathy for the common
people and their plight. His dislike for Madame Grandet, for example, is based in part on his revulsion at her refusal to contribute to a
drive to assist imprisoned but improperly clothed textile workers
being transported to Paris. And he considers Gauthier, the republican leader in Nancy, as one of the very few persons of integrity he
has encountered. Still, the numerous allusions to the republic in
Lucien Leuwen are not at all positive. Though attracted by the
integrity of the republicans, Lucien is repulsed by their singlemind-
edness. More importantly, in Stendhal's eyes, republicanism, in its
democratic form, leads to baseness. In one of his prefaces to the
novel he states, "The author would not want at all to live in a
democracy similar to that of America, for the simple reason that he
prefers to have to pay court to the minister of the interior than to the
neighborhood grocer" (*LL*, 1:2).

At the end of the novel Lucien reflects on American democracy
and considers that its government has fallen into the gutter opposite
that in which France finds itself. He believes that universal suffrage
reigns as a tyrant in America, that it puts one at the mercy of one's
shoemaker, who is likely to spread calumnies if he is not sufficiently
flattered. Lucien concludes, "Men are not evaluated, but counted,
and the vote of the most ill-mannered worker counts as much as that
of Jefferson and is often preferred" (*LL*, 4:312-13). Democratic
republicanism is but another form of tyranny for Stendhal, who per-

sonally favored an aristocracy of the mind. He frequently stated that if he had to choose between American-style political freedom and despotic elegance, he would choose elegance.

Stendhal has no illusions that the common people could one day save France. To the contrary, he is convinced that in elections the people will inevitably be taken in by the powerful, as the elections in the department of Cher and especially in Caen amply prove. Mairobert wins the election in Caen not because the electors in their wisdom have chosen the best man, which by all indications he is, but because the prefect, Monsieur de Séranville, has acted with utter stupidity. Stendhal clearly suggests that with new means of communication at their disposal, those in power will always be able to crush the opposition. How could the masses, who are even less intelligent that the electors of Caen, be able to overcome an unscrupulous government that has both money and the telegraph at its disposal?

Monsieur Leuwen's being elected a deputy by making all sorts of promises to his electors is but further proof. Once elected, he makes no effort to support enlightened and reasonable policies; rather, he brings together the most ignorant deputies from the South and supports the most absurd positions on the chamber floor. As a result, he becomes both famous and powerful. Stendhal thereby places in doubt the value of a parliamentary system, for he gives no indication that universal suffrage would produce deputies who are more intelligent than the group of ignoramuses whom Monsieur Leuwen directs. Since the legitimists live in the past, since the constitutional monarchy has produced but ministers and functionaries who are devious and corrupt, and since republicanism could only lead to the tyranny of the ignorant, we can conclude that this novel is not so much an indictment of a particular political system as it is an indictment of government as such.

Lucien tells his colonel that he has "the most serious objections to all forms of government" (*LL*, 1:130), and Monsieur Leuwen seems to reflect the author's views when he says, "Every government, even that of the United States, lies always and about everything" (*LL*, 3:154). Deception is endemic to the institution. *Lucien Leuwen* does not pretend to be a treatise on political science, and Stendhal is clearly more interested in the influence of political institutions on men and women than he is in the institutions themselves, but we can certainly draw from this text a profound mistrust of all government. The experience in government and politics forms part of Lucien's education in the ways of the world, teaches him the extent of his own abilities, and, not unimportantly, proves to him that none of this is as important as his love for Madame de Chasteller.

Emancipation

Lucien's problems with identity, self-revelation, and self-protection are complicated by his relationship to money in a world completely absorbed by it. Stendhal's desire to attract attention to what he considered an obsession of his times is revealed in one of the titles he had envisaged for this novel, *L'Orange de Malte* (The Orange of Malta), an expression that, in the slang of the time, meant "money."[3] We have already quoted Monsieur Leuwen to the effect that the banks were now running the state. Lucien notes as well that "in these times, when money is everything, when everything can be sold, what is there comparable to an immense fortune spent adroitly and cunningly" (*LL*, 4: 295). Lucien is clearly misplaced in such a world. His father's business does not interest him, for he disdains money as does Madame de Chasteller. Financial interests are never absent from Stendhal's works, but their obtrusive presence is even more striking in this novel in which the characters' language is sometimes beholden to metaphors drawn from the economic sphere. Money is not, however, always sought for itself; most often it is sought for reasons of vanity (Monsieur Leuwen, for whom money is a game, is a notable exception). In the reign of Louis-Philippe wealth is the primary measure of prestige. To reject money is, in a sense, to reject the values of one's times.

In this respect Lucien's relationship to his father is crucial. Monsieur Leuwen is presented as a jovial, witty, caustic, bon vivant who has lived to the full and, as a consequence, has a keen understanding of life. More importantly, he is devoted to his son and his son's welfare. Lucien may be the one who makes the decision to join the army, but it is his father who, through his influence, makes this possible and who later intervenes to prevent the colonel from harassing Lucien. And when Lucien deserts his post his father uses his prestige to make things right and then obtains a position for him at the Ministry of the Interior. Moreover, Lucien can afford to be impertinent to government ministers only because he is Monsieur Leuwen's son. His father not only provides him with unlimited financial resources but also feigns to give him full freedom as well. On Lucien's return from Nancy his father says to him, "I won't abuse the fact that I am your father in order to interfere with your plans; be free, my son" (*LL*, 3: 135). On the following page he insists that Lucien do exactly as he pleases. Lucien is the only one of Stendhal's characters to whom he has given such a generous, well-intentioned father.

Yet this loving, caring father who wants nothing more than his son's happiness clearly interferes with his son's life. After his return to Paris from Nancy, Lucien lets his father dictate his daily agenda – even down to the amount of time he is to spend at the opera each day. The father believes that the frivolous social agenda he imposes on his son will protect him from the charge of republicanism and Saint-Simonianism, whose adherents had the reputation of being serious and somber. The more Monsieur Leuwen takes over textually, however – toward the end of the novel more pages are devoted to him than to his son – the more he takes over Lucien's life as well. Although he claims to deplore Lucien's malleability, his proclamation of his son's freedom conceals a need to make Lucien more like himself. In his attempts to control his son, the elder Leuwen emerges as a second novelist, determining what his character will do next. There is no better example than his attempts to control his son's love life.

We know relatively early in the novel that Monsieur Leuwen has a low opinion of Lucien's prowess with women. When Lucien asks him for help in getting invited into the aristocratic drawing rooms of Nancy, his father uncharacteristically declines. Instead, he scoffs at Lucien and tells him, "*studiate la matematica*." This Italian expression is a swipe at Lucien's virility, for it is a truncated version of a sentence in Rousseau's *Confessions* in which the phrase "*Lascia le donne e studia la matematica*" (Forget women and study mathematics) is used by a prostitute who questions Rousseau's virility.[4] On Lucien's return from Nancy, his father insists that he date dancers from the opera.

It is Monsieur Leuwen, of course, who decides that Lucien will have an affair with Madame Grandet and who, when Madame Grandet is unresponsive, bargains for her sexual favors for his son in exchange for a ministry for her husband. This deal is unbeknownst to Lucien, who is devastated when he learns of it. Monsieur Leuwen, it seems, has only contributed further to Lucien's low self-esteem, for Lucien is now convinced that he is incapable of inspiring love on his own. Paradoxically, however, this manipulative incident has positive consequences because it leads Lucien to break from paternal control.

Throughout the novel Lucien has never ceased to marvel at his father's wisdom and knowledge of human nature. While in Nancy and bewildered by his feelings for Madame de Chasteller, he wonders what his father would do in such circumstances. Yet it is worth noting that when Lucien believes that Madame de Chasteller has betrayed him and faces the biggest crisis of his life, it is not of his father that he thinks but of his mother. His immediate thought is that he must go to Paris to see her. The narrator adds that "everything in the world had lost its importance to him; only two things remained: his mother and Madame de Chasteller" (*LL*, 3:131). And it is his mother whom he goes to see first, feeling, one assumes, that she will have an understanding of his situation that his father could not have. He may be mistaken in this, for his mother's first act is to offer him money – something his father would have been expected to do. When Lucien learns of his father's dealings with Madame Grandet, he recognizes that his father is like all other fathers, that he "wants to make me happy, but *in his way*, not in mine" (*LL*, 4:308). In seeking his son's happiness according to his own definition of how that happiness should occur, Monsieur Leuwen impedes Lucien's quest for an identity. The ideals of eighteenth-century worldliness to which he adheres do not mitigate his penchant for manipulating his son.

What had seemed an exceptional rehabilitation of fatherhood on Stendhal's part reveals itself to be a restatement from a different angle of the stultifying effects of fatherhood. As Lucien comes to see his father for what he is, the reader begins to distance himself from this engaging man, for his political machinations show him to be a man without ideas, a man whose political reputation is built on language that signifies nothing. His lack of trust in others, which may have seemed wise in earlier episodes, becomes distasteful when applied to his son. His amoral teachings, which seemed based on a superior wisdom, now appear as justifications for a cynical manipulation of others. When Lucien returns to Nancy to see Madame de

Chasteller, he is signaling to his father that his efforts to reform him have failed. Significantly, Monsieur Leuwen, having lost out in his efforts to convert his son to the ideals of worldliness, dies during Lucien's absence.

At the beginning of the novel Lucien is seeking to find what he is and what he is capable of. At the end of the novel he has grown considerably in self-knowledge and does know what he is capable of: "This stupid administrative work has at least proved to me that I am capable of earning my living and that of my wife" (*LL*, 4:313). Then he reflects that he does not have a high opinion of those to whom he has so proven and decides, "Well, . . . by God, it has proved it to me, and that is what's important" (*LL*, 4:313). What he is and what he is capable of no longer depend on the opinion of others but on his own assessment. He now separates himself from his father, takes a false name, and rents a furnished apartment, exclaiming, "Here, I am free" (*LL*, 4:315).

Lucien has proved to himself that he can earn his own living, but he has realized that he could not be himself without freeing himself from parental control. After his father's death, Lucien accepts to liquidate his father's debts, although he is not obligated to do so and this is not in his financial interest. It is, of course, a matter of honor, but it is also much more than that, for, as David Place has put it, Lucien is also settling a moral debt.[5] If he is to start living his own life, he must do so without any assistance from parental wealth. When the novel ends Lucien has finally attained an autonomy of self and therefore manhood. We need not be surprised that Stendhal did not write the third section.

An Unfinished Novel?

The novel that has come to be called *Lucien Leuwen* – that Stendhal at various points in its composition called *L'Orange de Malte*, *Le Bois de Prémol* (The Premol Woods), *Le Chasseur vert* (The Green Huntsman), and other titles as well – is a text that Stendhal never published. The idea for the novel came to him originally after reading the manuscript of a novel entitled *The Lieutenant*, by his friend Madame Jules Gaulthier, who had asked for his comments on it. His reaction was not favorable, and in a letter to Madame Gaulthier he severely criticized her work for its bombastic style, its pedestrian ending, its improper choice of names for the characters, and its insistence on telling the reader about passions instead of showing them. Madame Gaulthier's manuscript nonetheless inspired him, for the following day he began work on a novel with a similar subject.

Since his friend's manuscript no longer exists, it is not possible to determine what Stendhal might have drawn from it. He had projected a three-volume work, with the first volume set in Nancy, the second in Paris, and the third in Rome. He did write the first two, but not the third. In a note in 1835 he admitted that he had abandoned the idea for a third volume because he did not feel up to the task of writing a new exposition and creating still a new cast of characters. But there is still another reason that can explain why Stendhal did not write the third section as originally projected. The happy ending (Lucien was to return to France after a period as embassy secretary in Rome, meet Madame de Chasteller, and marry her) does not cohere with the clotural esthetics of Stendhal's novels, whereby the major characters are either eliminated or repaired to a monastery or nunnery. Because he did not attempt to publish the two volumes he did write, however, the novel is sometimes referred to as an "unfinished" novel. There is reason to dispute that claim.

In a letter to Sainte-Beuve in December 1834, Stendhal refers to the novel as containing sections on Nancy and Paris only. And in an 1835 letter to his editor, Alphonse Levavasseur, he mentions having completed a novel in two volumes. What is "unfinished" about the novel is not that the third volume was not written but that Stendhal, realizing that he could not publish the novel, neglected to put together a clean copy of the two parts he had intended to constitute the novel. As a consequence the names of secondary characters are confused on a few occasions, and toward the end of the Paris segment Lucien's visit to Nancy is not related. Stendhal did, however, consider the manuscript publishable, and he left instructions that, in the event of his death, his sister, his cousin Colomb, and his editor should remove allusions that are too obvious and clean up the style. But why not have had it published himself?

Lucien Leuwen is Stendhal's most political novel, and this fact more than anything else explains why he did not publish it during his lifetime. He was, as French consul in Civitavecchia, an official of the government and could not realistically have been expected to keep his position – which he needed financially – had he published a novel so scathing in its satire of the July Monarchy. The manuscript is loaded with precautionary anagrams such as "*téjé*" for *jésuite* and "Zogui" for Guizot (then a high government official). These puzzles are easily solved, and publishing the book in this form would not have been possible. In any case, some of the government figures in the novel were clearly based on current or former members of the government. The identities of their models were sometimes too clear. In a note Stendhal states, "As long as I have to serve the Budget in order to live, I won't be able to *print it*, for what the Budget hates the most, it's that someone pretend to have ideas" (*LL*, 4:359). By "Budget" Stendhal means the government. Of still more importance to Stendhal, the government, following an assassination attempt on the king, had put into place in September 1835 a number of repressive measures aimed at critics of the regime and severely curtailed freedom of the press. It is therefore no surprise that in concluding his second (1835) preface to the novel Stendhal cautioned, "If publication is imprudent because of the police, let us wait ten years" (*LL*, 1:5). Ten years later Stendhal was dead.

Chapter Five

The Life of Henry Brulard: The Incomplete Mosaic

The latter half of the eighteenth century had witnessed a multiplication of memoirs, the most important of which were Rousseau's *Confessions*, an unabashed self-revelation that constituted a revolution in the telling of the self. Prior to Rousseau, autobiographical writing had tended to be either self-accusatory (Augustine) or an exaltation of one's extraordinary personality (Cellini), or it consisted of memoirs of public figures who told of their participation in the major events of politics or history. Rousseau's is the first autobiography to attempt to give a comprehensive view of its author's personality. Boldly announcing that he will "bare his interior," Rousseau is quite conscious of the originality of his project: "I am embarking on an enterprise for which there is no previous example and whose execution will have no imitators."[1] Indeed, the term *autobiography* was introduced into critical discourse, according to Philippe Lejeune, to account for works such as Rousseau's, which, while presenting themselves as memoirs, had as a distinctive trait that their center of interest lay not in the political or historical events the author might have witnessed or in which he might have participated but rather in the story of the author's own intimate personality.[2] Stendhal, an avid reader of the *Confessions*, was clearly marked by them.

Stendhal's autobiographical inclinations first manifest themselves in a diary he sporadically kept from 1801 to 1823. The first paragraph of this journal affirms the principle of sincerity to which he will seek to adhere in all his autobiographical writings: "I take it as a principle not to be embarrassed and never to erase anything" (*J*, 1:3). He did make a few subsequent revisions and additions, however, and the sincerity he seeks does not preclude occasional attempts to deceive a potential reader. The author remains even in such a case sincere toward himself by marking the deception in some way – normally by inserting the deceptive material within parentheses. In the first years especially, the *Journal* limits itself to noting the people Stendhal has met, the books he has read, and the plays he has seen, as well as details on his military life, health, and financial problems. But beyond these banal details, we find in the *Journal* a strong inclination to self-analysis, the first evidence of a tendency to see himself as both subject and object. This penchant is also clear in his letters, especially those to his sister Pauline and in the margins of his books in which he habitually jots down reflections about himself and his times. This self-analysis sometimes contains retrospective commentary that brings the writing closer to the autobiographical genre proper. Already in the *Journal* we note Stendhal's conviction that understanding "the human heart" includes understanding oneself.

It comes as no surprise, then, that in 1832, when he was almost 50, Stendhal would yield to the autobiographical temptation. He began to write what he projected as an account of his life from 1821 to 1830 – that is, the period he spent in Paris after having left Milan and Mathilde. Titled *Mémoires d'égotisme* (*Memoirs of Egotism*), it is an account of the aftermath of his failed relationship with Mathilde. Shattered by her refusal but declining to speak or write about it, he relates how he was in constant fear that someone might discover his failure in love, how the memory of Mathilde rendered him temporarily impotent, how in order to forget her he frequented fashionable drawing rooms and traveled to London, and how he befriended the Italian opera singer Madame Pasta in order to hear Mathilde's language spoken. Like *On Love*, this is a book haunted by Mathilde. Stendhal worked on the manuscript only a couple of weeks, however, writing what amounts to 100 pages or so in most editions, and then ceased writing well before the narrative reached the year 1830 as he had planned. It is not clear why he stopped, but from the beginning he had been uncomfortable with the project: "I feel . . . a real repugnance at writing solely to talk about myself" (*ME*, 4). It may very well be that he found it particularly difficult to deal with a period of his life that was still relatively recent and would have included his relationship with Clémentine Curial.

Three years later, however, he began once again to write his life. Entitled *Vie de Henry Brulard* (*The Life of Henry Brulard*), this account begins with his childhood. He is still very much concerned about putting himself on display and particularly troubled about how to write about himself without constantly repeating the first-person pronoun. He especially wants to avoid the kind of self-centeredness he found in the work of Chateaubriand, who is a major negative reference for his writing. The other major reference is Rousseau, but here the relationship is more ambiguous. Although he does not want to write like him, he recognizes Rousseau's greatness and feels awkward about criticizing the *Confessions*: "I'll be seen as envious, or rather as seeking to establish a comparison, appalling in its absurdity, with the masterpiece of that great writer" (*HB*, 2: 63). Stendhal's recognition of the importance and originality of the *Confessions* did not prevent him, however, from producing a work that is markedly different from Rousseau's.

In their respective works, Rousseau and Stendhal differ sharply in how they deal with their past and current identities. As Richard N. Coe has pointed out, Rousseau is wont to use his great stylistic gifts to detrivialize his youth and render it important.[3] Stendhal is not always sure of the importance or even the interest that his childhood might have, but he refuses to have recourse to literary style in order to make these childhood events seem less banal. More significantly, Rousseau is confident that he knows the truth about himself and his past: "Let the trumpet of the last judgment sound when it wishes. I shall come, this book in hand, to present myself to the sovereign judge. I'll say loudly: here is what I did, what I thought, what I was" (Rousseau, 4). Stendhal has no such certitude about himself and his past. He is unsure whether he has had any control over his life and is the first to admit that he does not know who or what he is. Jean Prévost has pointed out that when Rousseau begins his autobiography, he does it deliberately, having looked at himself and his past and having judged himself favorably, while for Stendhal, the internal debate continues throughout the autobiography (Prévost, 316). Forgoing Rousseau's project of self-justification (there are few moments of repentance for personal failings in this text), Stendhal is the first to use this genre to explore the question of the identity of the self and the uncertain possibilities of its discovery through writing. Rather than a presentation of the self to others, it is a seeking of one's own essence.

A few years earlier, when writing *Memoirs of Egotism*, he had asked himself, "What kind of man am I? Do I have good sense? Do I have a remarkable mind? In truth, I don't know" (*ME*, 3-4). The lack of sure self-knowledge troubled him: "I don't know myself and that's what, sometimes, when I think about it at night, distresses me" (*ME*, 5). The search for self-knowledge evident in *Memoirs of Egotism* informs *The Life of Henry Brulard* as well. The first pages, a meditation on Rome seen from Mount Janiculum, juxtaposes, as Victor Brombert has noted, historical and personal time (Brombert, 10). As the quinquagenarian author contemplates both modern and ancient Rome, he is faced with physical evidence of the flux of time. Significantly, his meditation is in the interrogative mood. The opening is marked not by affirmations but by doubt: "I'm going to be fifty years old; it would be time for me to know myself. What have I been? What am I? In truth, I would be very hard pressed to say" (*HB*, 1: 4). This interrogative mood sets the stage for a continued questioning. Still, 250 pages later he does not seem to have progressed much on the path of self-knowledge: "But fundamentally, dear reader, I don't know what I am: good, bad, witty, stupid" (*HB*, 2: 122). This consciousness of the fleeting nature of his own character, of the elusiveness of human personality, renders *The Life of Henry Brulard* resolutely modern. Writing his life is Stendhal's attempt to capture at least a few aspects of this unseizable personality: "I don't pretend in the least to be writing a history; rather I am simply noting my memories in order to guess at what kind of a man I've been. This is the answer to that great saying: Know thyself" (*HB*, 2: 13).

Stendhal is further aware that his past personality does not entirely cohere with his current one: "I'm so different than I was twenty years ago that I seem to be making discoveries about someone else" (*HB*, 2: 273). He is quite capable of laughing at that someone else, gently making fun of his enjoyment of a certain landscape, which, he now thinks, was probably not any good, of his adolescent ideas regarding his own genius, or his adolescent belief that he was both a Saint-Preux and a Valmont. There are aspects of the human personality, he understands, that are discontinuous. The more important character traits, however, are remarkable for their persistence. Early in the book he affirms that "forty-five years ago, my manner of seeking happiness was exactly what it is today; in other words, my character was absolutely the same as today" (*HB*, 1: 164). Later he exclaims, in English, "I am still in 1835 the man of 1794" (*HB*, 1: 243). *The Life of Henry Brulard* acknowledges change in behavior but testifies to a more important permanence in the self.

In *Memoirs of Egotism* Stendhal had recognized writing as a process of self-discovery: "It's only in reflecting in order to be able to write this that what was going on in my heart in 1821 becomes clear to my eyes" (*ME*, 19). In *The Life of Henry Brulard*, in which he makes a more serious attempt to recover the vestiges of his past, impressions he thought he had forgotten now rise to the surface: "Many things come back to me while writing" (*HB*, 1: 204); "it's astounding how many things I'm remembering since I've been writing these Confessions. They come all at once" (*HB*, 2: 126); "I've made great discoveries about myself in writing these *Memoirs*" (*HB*, 2: 169). The very act of writing provides an opportunity to grasp some of the elusive strands of his personality, though Stendhal is acutely aware that the whole personality can never be recovered.

In contrast to Rousseau, then, Stendhal does not know the truth about himself and his past. That truth, if it is to be attained at all, is to be discovered by the act of writing. Moreover, as notes in the margins of his manuscript attest, he realized that the more rapidly he wrote, the more fragments of reality he would discover. As a result of this deliberate pace, the entire manuscript was written in 14 weeks. Richard N. Coe has remarked that "it is almost as though, the better part of a century before Breton and Soupault, he had discovered the principle of automatic writing – speed, in this case, furnishing the element of automatism" (Coe, 29).

In such a project, the role of memory becomes highly important but also highly problematic. *Memoirs of Egotism* had been filled with expressions such as "I have no recollection how" (*ME*, 71) and "I don't know what brought me to" (*ME*, 147), and *The Life of Henry Brulard* abounds in similar expressions. As he writes, Stendhal is aware that some facts have faded, that he is presenting but "their shadow" (*HB*, 1: 248) and that he is probably mistaken about them. He knows, for example, that in sketching a person's character he has to be influenced by those character traits of that person which he has recognized later rather than the traits he might have perceived at the time he is writing about. He realizes that all kinds of things posterior to an event will influence the way he now views the event. About a childhood injury he has just related, he notes, "I picture the event, but probably this is not a direct memory; it's but the memory of the image which I formed of the thing long ago at the time when it was first related to me" (*HB*, 1: 75). Referring to his descent from

Mount Saint Bernard, he notes, "I don't want to hide the fact that five or six years afterwards, I saw an engraving of it which I thought quite accurate, and my memory now is *only* of the engraving" (*HB*, 2: 345). Memories can never render the past perfectly, for they are invariably clouded by more recent thoughts and feelings. No writer before Stendhal seems to have been so conscious of the traps of memory.

Still, we have no choice but to rely on memory. As V. Del Litto has shown, one of the most daring and modern aspects of this autobiography is the way in which Stendhal understands memory.[4] Unlike previous memorialists and autobiographers, Stendhal avoids representing the past as a monolithic block. One critic has very pertinently pointed out the rhetorical importance of beginning the narrative with a contemplation of a city, Rome, that is inseparable from its historical traces.[5] We can form an idea of Rome only through its vestiges. So, too, perhaps for an individual. Personal traces, however, are more difficult to recover than architectural ones, for memory is unreliable and inconsistent. The image Stendhal uses to represent this insight is drawn from the world of medieval art: "Next to the clearest of images, I find deficiencies in memory; it's like a fresco from which large pieces have fallen" (*HB*, 1: 178). The image of the damaged fresco was dear to him, for he reused it several times to illustrate his faltering memory. The act of writing, sometimes functioning like Proustian "involuntary memory," assisted him in salvaging some of the fallen pieces of fresco. It is not always memory that makes writing possible; sometimes it is writing that makes memory possible. In trying to re-create his previous self, Stendhal has become sensitive to the very process of memory, to the operations of memory, and to its relationship to experience.

Memory's unreliability does present problems for the autobiographer who prizes sincerity: "But how many precautions does one have to take in order not to lie?" (*HB*, 1: 13); "all my explanations may be faulty" (*HB*, 1: 71). Conscious of the pitfalls of autobiography, he therefore writes a text that is partly a critique of the genre as it was then understood. When Stendhal hopes to "be true" he is not referring to objective exactitude. What is important for him is not the truth of events but rather the truth of his reactions to events: "I protest anew that I am not pretending to depict things as they are in themselves, but only their effect on me" (*HB*, 1: 214). It is what he felt that he is most interested in recording. When he recounts how his father had been denounced as being politically suspect, he adds that, by doing research in the departmental archives, it might be possible to contradict some of his facts but he is certain of the effect on himself and his family (*HB*, 1: 170). The real self of *The Life of Henry Brulard* is not the historical, the political, or even the intellectual self; it is the affective self.

Concentrating on the affective self, however, is not without danger. How is it possible to prevent such a narrative from becoming pure fantasy? In both *Memoirs of Egotism* and *The Life of Henry Brulard* Stendhal reminds himself that he needs to check archives for dates of birth and death and other events, but he also attempts to recover objectivity by situating himself spatially and placing events in a material context. This would appear to be the purpose of his numerous drawings that illustrate various settings and events in *The Life of Henry Brulard*. Philippe Lejeune has proposed that this book in which there is a constant interaction between the writing and the approximately 170 drawings is a kind of bilingual text in which the drawings assist in telling the story in another semiotic system (Lejeune, 31). The drawings are almost always topographical sketches, frequently giving the author's spatial location at the time of the narrated event, accompanied by commentary.

It is not clear what would have happened to the illustrations if Stendhal had decided to publish the manuscript, for these sketches, which sometimes seem to engender themselves,[6] would seem to assist the writer more than the reader, who may be more confused than helped by them. The act of drawing has the function of capturing the writer's memory of an event by situating it spatially. The drawing obviates description ("I abhor material description" [*ME*, 49]) and thereby the necessity of making "literature," thus contributing to the speed of the process. Stendhal's textual references to surrounding objects such as Abbé Raillane's canary cage might have a similar purpose. Through the drawings and the objects, Stendhal avoids the danger of wandering off into the realm of the imagination. His interior life thereby unfolds as a function of an exterior life that is real.

Henri Martineau made the pertinent observation that Stendhal was one of the first to express the sentiments of his heart according to a logic not of time but of memory.[7] The rhythm of memory, however, does not produce a linear, chronological structure, and consequently the work is fragmented. Incidents are recounted that have no obvious relationships with the others being told. Characters appear briefly, then disappear for good. The narrator repeats himself and is prone to digression – a habit he himself acknowledges as early as chapter 1: "But I'm wandering off again" (*HB*, 1:15). The reader is struck by a sense of discontinuity, especially given the brackets, ellipses, italics, and snippets of English and Italian. The whole gives the impression of spontaneity, creating a rhythm that is not, however, inappropriate to autobiography as the genre has come to be understood since Stendhal. The effect gives the reader the impression that he is not reading a finished product but witnessing the creation of a text.

That rhythm includes important gaps in the narration. The author begins to relate an event, a duel he had in his adolescence, for example, but does not explain why or how it ended because he cannot remember. Stendhal is constantly resisting what must have been a strong temptation, especially for a novelist, to fill in the gaps and thus assure the continuity of the narrative. Rousseau, for his part, admitted to filling in the gaps.[8] When Stendhal remembers but a fragment of an event, however, that is all the reader gets. He is aware of these narrative truncations, explaining at one point, "I would be lying and making a novel if I undertook to give more detail" (*HB*, 2:361).[9] By deliberately writing for readers of the future whose cultural references he cannot know, he believes he is guarding himself against the temptation to depict himself favorably by embellishing his story. This does not mean that there are no fictionalizations, no dramatizations whatsoever. Indeed, the work begins with a fictionalization: Stendhal was not in Rome at the time that, in the opening pages of the book, he claims to have been there. What is important for Stendhal is that he yield as little as possible to the temptation to fictionalize, that *The Life of Henry Brulard* not become a novel.

Although Stendhal claims not to believe in children who "give promise of becoming superior men" (*HB*, 1:55), he manages to attribute a destiny to his own childhood. This boy who struggles against his enemies within his milieu is marked with the energy of which heroes are constituted. Precocious in his denunciation of hypocrisy and tyranny and endowed with adult qualities, this child is clearly out of the ordinary. The 20 engravings, most of biblical subjects, that Stendhal interspersed in his manuscript may be an effort as well to point to a destiny.[10] When Stendhal repeats that he does not want to "novelize" his life, he refers to his decision not to add anything to what his memory reveals, not to elaborate artistically on his childhood adventures. It does not mean that he is able to escape – or even wants to escape – from the rules of narrative that call for events to contribute to the fashioning of character.

Can we, however, speak of an autobiography when only the author's childhood and adolescence are told? Richard N. Coe has suggested that *The Life of Henry Brulard* is the first great example of a particular type of autobiography – a subspecies of the genre that has by now become well-known and that might be called "memories of childhood and youth" (Coe, 29). This subgenre, whose French twentieth century practitioners include Pierre Drieu la Rochelle, Gide, Julien Green, Michel Leiris, and Sartre, has its own definition and rules. It is a writing about the experience of the author during childhood and adolescence, presented in chronological order but according to the rhythm of this experience. The narrative always ends when maturity has been attained, when "a past identity . . . is transformed into something with which, at the moment of writing, [the author] can identify" (Coe, 30).

Stendhal ends his own narrative a few days after his arrival in Italy in 1801. We know that those days were an important turning point in his life, that they constituted for him the moment at which he attained maturity. In the memoirs of the seventeenth and eighteenth centuries, childhood and adolescence, in the rare cases where they were recounted at all, served as an introduction to the important part of the narration that was the life of the adult. Rousseau, however, had expressed, especially in his *Emile*, the view that the child's mind is autonomous, with its own structures and ways of understanding. The child is not an imperfect adult but rather a being with his own capacities. Rousseau broke with his predecessors by considerably enlarging the attention given to childhood and youth, and, in his *Confessions*, the part dealing with his youth occupies one-third of the volume. Yet even in Rousseau childhood remains a kind of introduction to the story of adulthood. There is no moment in Rousseau's text that could be identified as a turning point.

One of Rousseau's contributions to the literature of childhood was his recognition that sexual experience begins earlier than had been theretofore believed. While Stendhal does not indulge in reve-lations about his adolescent sexuality, his awakening to desire (e.g., toward his aunt Camille Poncet) is very much present. He also reveals the main object of his desire: his mother. On this issue Den-nis Porter has suggested that there is no author prior to Freud who wrote more directly than did Stendhal on the Oedipal triangle,[11] even if, in Stendhal's case, the love for the mother is not repressed. Indeed, the passages on his love for his mother, who died in child-birth when he was seven, are striking by their explicitness: "I was in love with my mother. . . . I wanted to cover my mother with kisses and that she have no clothes on. . . . I always wanted to kiss her on the breast" (*HB*, 1: 44). Given the intensity of this love, it is no sur-prise that the most traumatic event related in this autobiography is the death of the mother. As Béatrice Didier has pointed out, the first direct quotations of himself as a child relate to his reactions to his mother's death.[12] It is here that his memory seems to be the sharpest: "The entire dialogue of that night is still present to me. I could transcribe it right here" (*HB*, 1: 54). Stendhal dates the begin-ning of his "moral life" from that moment which might also be seen as the beginning of a life-long attempt to recapture the happiness associated with his idyllic existence prior to his mother's death. A number of problematics of Stendhal's work can be traced to this complex, particularly the relations between father and son.

It is in this context that the title of the book is best understood. For, how are we to explain that the title of this autobiography con-tains a name which is not that of the author? Where does the name Brulard come from? Stendhal writes, "My uncle kidded his sister Henriette (my mother) about my ugliness. It appears that I had a large head, no hair, and that I resembled Father Brulard, an astute monk, a bon vivant with considerable influence in his monastery, my uncle or great uncle who died before I was born" (*HB*, 1: 74). Throughout his life Stendhal was very sensitive about his supposed ugliness. His choice of the name Brulard is clearly a way to affirm that unattractiveness while making fun of it. *Brulard*, as Dennis Porter has pointed out, is a word whose root is negated by its suffix (Porter, 159). "Brul," with its relation to the French verb *brûler*, "to burn," would signify ardor and a certain Romantic intensity. On the other hand, the ending "ard" is comic and slightly pejorative in French. But there is more to this title than humorous self-deprecation, for we also know that Stendhal had a propensity for pseudonyms, having used more than 200 during his lifetime. Jean Starobinski has seen in this an act of protest. Taking on a pseudonym, he points out, is a manner of repudiating the father, whose name Stendhal rejects, as well as the father's values.[13] This seems valid in light of the hostile relationship that is recounted in this text between Stendhal and his father.

The opposition to the father, also a feature of Chateaubriand's autobiography, may owe something to the rules of narrative (Didier, 44), and its formulation may have clear literary antecedents,[14] but the entries in the *Journal* in the early 1800s bear witness to the seriousness of the conflict. In the autobiography Stendhal expressed his conviction that his father did not love him as an individual but only as a son who would perpetuate the family. He was persuaded that he had a character completely opposite that of his father: "Never before perhaps has chance brought together two beings more thoroughly opposed to each other than my father and I" (*HB*, 1: 107). In relation to his mother, he was "in the depths of [his] soul, jealous of [his] father" (*HB*, 1: 189). In general, he considered his father to be a tyrant and a hypocrite, and he extended his hatred for his father to his father's city, religious beliefs, and political allegiance. Indeed, the child's precocious historical and political consciousness – a feature original to this autobiography – is explained as a reaction against the historical and political views of his family.

Decades later, Stendhal's hostility toward his father remained unabated. At no point does he attempt to understand his father who, the evidence would suggest, seems to have been a decent man who suffered the loss of his young wife very deeply. Given Stendhal's implacable hostility toward him, it is not improbable that the pseudonym functions as a repudiation mechanism. The repudiation of the father, moreover, has strong implications for the freedom of the son. Is to reject the father's name not a means of rejecting all predestination associated with being the father's son? Could it be that the author, as Victor Brombert has suggested, is seeking to become his own creator? (Brombert, 9). Lucien Leuwen, as we have seen in the last chapter, seems to find his own identity only when he adopts a pseudonym. *The Life of Henry Brulard* is, then, a restate-ment of a conflict central to Stendhal's fiction.

In the personal mythology he created for himself, Stendhal had an idyllic childhood until his mother's death. Afterwards, he had a "black and white" childhood, with the members of his family divided between the good (his grandfather, his great aunt Elizabeth, his uncle Romain Gagnon, and his sister Pauline) and the bad (his father, his aunt Séraphie, Abbé Raillane, and his sister Zénaïde). The reader can detect that the cleavage between these two groups was not absolute and that all members of the family took pride in his youthful accomplishments, but these were real divisions for the child. Stendhal quickly concluded that his family was hypocritical, and he even claimed to like mathematics in part because "hypocrisy was impossible in mathematics" (*HB*, 2: 20). His own hypocrisy he excuses as a necessary defense against a tyrannical family. He justi-fies his deception by asking, "Is lying not the only resource of slaves?" (*HB*, 1: 228). The adult Stendhal is aware that this Manichaean childhood influenced his personality. Not being allowed by his "tyrants" to play with children his age led, in his judgment, to his timidity, naïveté, and romantic ideas. For Stendhal, childhood has a determining effect on the formation of the adult.

Stendhal considered himself extremely sensitive, but he claims to have always attempted to hide this sensitivity from others. "Love," he writes at one point, "has always been for me the most important of things" (*HB*, 2: 61). And it is precisely of love that he was never able to speak to anyone: "I'm taken, I believe, for the most cheerful and insensitive of men; it's true that I've never said a single word about the women I loved" (*HB*, 1: 19). He has consistently tried to protect his sensitivity: "I've never spoken," he writes, "about what I adored; such words would have seemed to me blasphemy" (*HB*, 1: 253); "during my entire life, I've never spoken of the thing for which I was the most impassioned; the slightest objection would have pierced my heart" (*HB*, 1: 277).

It is not difficult to see why he never spoke of Mathilde, about whom he still thinks 10 times a week. Yet this extreme discretion regarding his own happiness made it difficult for him to give an unbroken narrative of his life. He had already faced this problem in *Memoirs of Egotism*: "I feared that I might deflower the moments of happiness that I've had by describing them, by anatomizing them"

(*ME*, 5). His solution? "I will skip the happiness" (*ME*, 5). Like the mystics who are aphasic about their ecstasy, like Rousseau who found himself incapable of describing his joy at Les Charmettes, Stendhal cannot speak or write about what has moved him the most (although he did come close in his description of his idyllic visit to Les Echelles). The inability or unwillingness to write about his happiness in Milan in 1801 is certainly a major reason for his ending *The Life of Henry Brulard*. The last pages of the book reflect this dilemma: "How can I depict such crazy happiness?" (*HB*, 2: 371); "my God, I can't continue; the subject surpasses the telling of it" (*HB*, 2: 372). The last line reads, "Such tender feelings are spoiled when related in detail" (*HB*, 2: 373).

Some critics have proposed that Stendhal stopped writing *The Life of Henry Brulard* because he had just been granted a leave permitting him to return to Paris. It can be more plausibly argued that the book ends when Stendhal realizes that there are things that cannot be recounted, that there are experiences of such great moment that they ought not be tarnished by being told.

Chapter Six

Tales of Action

Stendhal and Short Fiction

While Stendhal is better known as a novelist than as a writer of short stories, his interest in short fiction was considerable and can be traced to the earliest stages of his career. Practically all his nonfiction contains anecdotes that, though often only a few lines long, are embryonic short stories. His first published work, *The Lives of Haydn, Mozart, and Metastasio*, contains, for example, an anecdote about a seventeenth-century singer and his mistress that is then retold in a more developed fashion in *The Life of Rossini*. A few of these anecdotes are long enough to stand as short stories in their own right. An example would be the story of Ernestine, which Stendhal wrote for an anticipated second edition of *On Love*. Written in 1822 and 1825, it is Stendhal's first piece of short fiction. While its purpose is didactic (to illustrate the stages of crystallization), it is a complete short story that details the growth of the love of a young woman for an older man.

Stendhal began writing short stories as such around 1829-30, when the genre was beginning to affirm itself in France. Printing improvements had led to the expansion of newspapers, which, bolstered by advertising, were in a position to pay relatively decent prices for fiction. Stendhal was certainly in need of money and may also have been influenced in this direction by his younger friend, Prosper Mérimée, who was in the process of building a reputation for himself as a short-story writer. In any case, writing short fiction seems a natural outlet for someone who for years had been fascinated by anecdotes.

Most of Stendhal's energies and his best accomplishments in this domain deal with Italian subject matter, but a few pieces of short fiction with a non-Italian subject matter, all written around 1830, merit some attention. Appearing in *La Revue de Paris* in 1830, "Le Coffre et le Revenant" (The Chest and the Ghost) is a story of passion and murder and the only one of Stendhal's narratives set in Spain. The powerful head of the police, Don Blas Bustos, falls in love with Dona Ines and forces her to marry him by having her fiancé, Fernando, jailed and by threatening further harm to him unless she abides by his wishes. Through a contrived plot that includes his being smuggled into her room in a chest, Fernando does eventually succeed in making contact with Ines, but this leads only to her murder by the jealous Don Blas. A character who has been cruelly treated and who enjoys mistreating others, Don Blas is also an ugly man fascinated by the physical beauty of others, which he must either repress (he has Don Fernando jailed) or possess (he forcibly marries Ines). Ines is one of those female characters for whom Stendhal has a particular affection: she is a woman with deep religious faith who loves even when she believes that this love will lose her soul.

Also appearing in *La Revue de Paris* the same year was a tale based on a seventeenth-century story by Paul Scarron that Stendhal entitled "Le Philtre" (The Potion). It too is a tale of passion, this time leading to suicide. Léonore leaves her husband for a circus horseback rider whom she knows to be unreliable but whom she continues to love even after he has stolen her money and used that money to run off with another woman and to pay another man to sleep with her. Although her husband, though older and somewhat jealous, loves her and treats her well, Léonore continues to love the circus rider – an infatuation she attributes to his having made her drink a love potion. Yet Liéven, the young lieutenant to whom she tells this tale, becomes as passionately in love with her as she with her horseman, although he knows she loves another and could never love him. There is, then, no need of a potion to explain inexplicable love, for the rules of passion defy those of rationality. Liéven cannot face not being loved by Léonore and commits suicide in her arms. The only way she can respond is to enter a convent. The abrupt ending, typical of much of Stendhal's fiction, is his own invention, not Scarron's.

Around this same time Stendhal wrote another story, "Mina de Vanghel," which he did not publish. He had given some thought to expanding this story into a novel, but the text we have can stand on its own as a complete short story. It centers on a young German woman named Mina de Vanghel who, after her father's death, goes to live in France. There she falls in love with a married man, Monsieur de Larçay, and proceeds through various stratagems to convince him to leave his wife. When she later admits to him that she had staged the event that had convinced him that his wife was cheating on him, he leaves her in disgust. She in turn commits suicide for, the narrator tells us, "her soul was too filled with fire for her to be content with the reality of life" (*S*, 212).

This young woman's resourcefulness, cunning, and single-mindedness of purpose are striking to be sure. She is capable of manipulating others, as she does when she shamelessly gets Count Ruppert to court Madame de Larçay by promising to marry him within the year. That Ruppert could have been killed in this process (he was, in fact, wounded in a duel with Larçay) does not concern her much, for in her eyes he is but a fop whom she intends to buy off when she no longer needs him. Like a number of other female characters in Stendhal's fiction, Mina is stronger than the men she encounters. Her courage, like Mathilde's, is sustained and inspired by her ancestors, whom she addresses directly at one difficult point: "Spirits of my ancestors . . . like you I have courage. . . . I will be faithful to honor. That secret flame of honor and heroism that you have transmitted to me finds nothing worthy of itself in this prosaic century where destiny has left me" (*S*, 175). Her affinity for the life of her ancestors reemerges a few pages later: "My ancestors left their magnificent castle at Königsberg to go to the Holy Land; a few years later, they returned alone, facing innumerable dangers, disguised as I am. The courage which sustained them places me in the midsts of the only dangers which remain, in this puerile, boring, and vulgar century, for someone of my sex" (*S*, 177). Like a number of other Stendhalian characters, Mina has constructed for herself a morality built on her own understanding of what constitutes personal greatness. Stendhal was clearly fascinated by this story and several years later, in 1837, he worked on a longer version, "Le Rose et le Vert" ("The Pink and the Green"), but never completed it.

"Vanina Vanini"

All Stendhal's nonfiction relating to Italy includes anecdotes dealing with Italian life and mores, usually emphasizing individual energy and passion. His *Life of Rossini* contains such stories; *Rome, Naples, and Florence* incorporates even more, especially in the second edition of 1826; and *Walks in Rome* contains an even larger number. In 1829, one year after the publication of *Walks in Rome*, Stendhal published "Vanina Vanini," his first independent story on an Italian theme. Appearing in *La Revue de Paris*, it is based on a political situation then attracting considerable attention – namely, the revolutionary activity being carried out in Italy. The story's first sentence draws attention to the fact that the action takes place in the 1820s, and the subtitle, "Details of the Last Vente of Carbonari Discovered in the Papal States" (a *vente* was a revolutionary cell), situates it in a contemporary context.

The story begins with the description of a ball held by a wealthy banker who is also a duke. The newness of his palace indicates a current prosperity – a fact confirmed by his being able to put on a ball that no European king would be able to match. What is striking in the first two pages or so, however, is the contrast of events. At the same time the duke-banker is giving an expensive ball and his wealthy and noble guests are preoccupied with determining who is the most beautiful woman present, a carbonaro is escaping from Sant' Angelo prison. The power structure of contemporary Italy is under attack and may be vulnerable, since its prisons seem incapable of holding those who contest it. Indeed, the nobility itself may be losing its coherence. There are, to be sure, nobles such as Livio Savelli who are superficial, do not like to read, and are completely disinterested in politics. Others, however – like Countess Vittelleschi, who initially saves the carbonaro, Missirilli, and Don Asdrubal, Vanina's father, who harbors Missirilli in his home for four months – while not renouncing their class (Don Asdrubal, for one, is quite keen that his daughter marry within her class), come to the aid of revolutionaries for reasons that are unstated but that might be presumed to be patriotic.

Vanina Vanini, who gives her name to the title, is one of a number of strong women in Stendhal's work. Like Mathilde de la Mole, she denounces the vanity of the men of her class and prefers men of action. Whereas Mathilde had proclaimed that being condemned to death alone was meritorious, Vanina, when asked by Livio Savelli who could possibly please her, answers, "That young carbonaro who has just escaped; at least he has done something other than be born" (*S*, 56). She falls in love with a commoner, the political revolutionary Missirilli. As with Mathilde, Vanina's love for such a man allows her to take refuge in historical myths, at one point saying to Missirilli, "You are a great man like the ancient Romans" (*S*, 56). Like Mathilde, she is the one who makes the first declaration of love, and it is she who offers herself in marriage to Missirilli. Finally, she is quite willing to dishonor herself for the man she loves: "My lot from now on is to dare everything. . . . I'll lose myself for you, but no matter. Will you be able to love a woman so dishonored?" (*S*, 57). Her love is marked by a cerebral quality, by a calculation that Missirilli *owes* her his love because of what she has done for him. Thus she is able to betray his group, thinking thereby to save him for herself. Her miscalculation on this score leads to her being rejected by the man she loves and returned to the class that is her own but that she disdains.

Though considerably less developed, Missirilli is in many ways, a Cornelian character, torn between the conflicting demands of love and duty. In realizing his duty to his country, he can be spontaneous and impulsive, but his revolutionary activity is also a thoughtful, reasoned decision. The freedom for which he is fighting and for which he is willing to lay down his life is more important to him than the love of the most desirable woman of Rome – even when he is certain that this woman also loves him passionately. It is this ultimate commitment that Vanina fails to comprehend.

The story's ending is an unusual one for Stendhal. While the precipitous closure is hardly surprising in a Stendhalian text, one would have expected Vanina to either enter a convent or commit suicide. It is, of course, possible to interpret her marriage to Livio Savelli as a kind of suicide, but an alternative reading might interpret her continued life in the world as a sign that hers was not a true passionate love. She and Mathilde de la Mole are the only two of Stendhal's lovers who neither die nor enter a convent when they find themselves prevented from pursuing their love. Significantly, Stendhal reports the marriage in one terse, concluding sentence without any clue to the heroine's sentiments.

Italian Chronicles

In 1833, while Stendhal was French consul at Civitavecchia, the Caetani family placed at his disposition numerous manuscripts conserved at its residence in Rome. These manuscripts, which probably date from the seventeenth century, purport to relate true stories of the Italian Renaissance, a period that had long piqued Stendhal's curiosity. He took a keen interest in them and had a number copied for his future use. In the fall of 1834 he conceived the idea of publishing some of them in a volume to be entitled *Histoirettes romaines* (Little Roman Stories). Nothing came of this project, but in 1836, while he was on leave in Paris, he began transcribing and adapting some of these tales for publication in *La Revue des Deux Mondes*. He realized that his position as French consul at Civitavecchia precluded his using some of the materials, which would be too compromising for families now important in the Papal States, but he did have a number of manuscripts from which to choose. Those he selected might have minor political liabilities, and it is perhaps for this reason that he published them either anonymously or under the pseudonym Lagenevais. These have become known as the *Chroniques italiennes* (*Italian Chronicles*), a title chosen by Romain Colomb, Stendhal's cousin and literary executor, who published them under that title in 1855 as part of Stendhal's collected works.

The first of these, "Vittoria Accoramboni," appeared in 1837. Of all the Italian chronicles it adheres most closely to the Italian text, even to the point of occasionally imitating its flowery style. This is a tale devoid of unity that leaves unanswered many questions raised by the plot. Vittoria Accoramboni's husband has been murdered, but we are never told who committed the crime. Rumors are reported, but none are confirmed. Vittoria's remarriage to Prince Orsini lends suspicion to his involvement, but no proof is ever brought forth. The role of Cardinal Montalto, later to become Pope Sixtus V, is never revealed. Much space is given to the manner in which Montalto reacts to the murder of his nephew, with the narrator clearly in admiration of his self-control and powers of dissimulation, but he then drops out of the narrative for good. Vittoria Accoramboni is later cruelly murdered without the identity of her attackers being clearly revealed. The indications are that she was killed by Orsini's brother with the agreement of Orsini's son by a previous marriage, but then another man is executed for the crime. This narrative might be read as a subverted detective story, for while crimes are committed, clues abound, and suspects are identified, none of the puzzles is fully explained at the end.

It is clear that in telling this story Stendhal was interested in neither a well-constructed plot nor a probing analysis of character; rather, he wished to create a climate of vengeance, violence, and crime. He considered the more passionate and instinctual mores of the Italian Renaissance to be a healthy antidote to the effete social habits of his own time. Seeking to put his readers in touch with another kind of humanity, Stendhal is at pains in the first few paragraphs to recall the otherness of Italian life in 1585 as he stresses the lack of affectation and vanity in that culture. By depicting mores that are vastly different but that in their time and place appear completely normal, he is raising the question of the relativity of morals, with which he had dealt a number of times in his essays.

"Les Cenci" ("The Cenci"), also published in 1837 in *La Revue des Deux Mondes*, relates a story that had long interested Stendhal – that of the 16-year-old Béatrice Cenci, who, after repeated sexual assaults by her father, participates in his murder. The story maintains the atmosphere of the previous tale, giving Stendhal once again the opportunity to present mores that were altogether different from those of nineteenth-century France. The characters in this story, much like those of the previous one, are quite ready to affirm their individual selves. François Cenci, who cruelly abuses his wife and forces his daughter into incest as well as other "unspeakable loves" (which the Italian manuscript identifies as sodomy), does whatever he pleases regardless of the consequences. While not admiring these sins and crimes, Stendhal seems to be fascinated with the strength of personality and the strangeness of character that lie behind them.

The description of Cenci, which is totally of Stendhal's invention, mentions that he is "too thin," that his upper eyelids "drooped a bit too much," and that his nose was "too long and too big" (*IC*, 1: 57). This quadruple use of *too* signals the larger-than-life character of Cenci and may also, as one Italian critic has suggested, be a way of stressing difference and deviance.[1] Though but a teenager, Béatrice reveals exceptional inner strength. When the two outlaws she and her mother have hired to kill her father declare themselves incapable of accomplishing the deed, she reveals her disdain for them, announcing that she will do the job herself. Likewise, she is steadfast under police torture and goes to her death serenely and with dignity. It seems appropriate that she should be buried beneath Raphael's painting of the Transfiguration (a detail added by Stendhal). She too must be listed among the women of strong character who people Stendhal's fiction.

Stendhal's interest in depicting a society in which more primal urges rise to the surface does not entail a willingness to relate all their consequences in detail. Although he describes the horrible manner in which Cenci is murdered (by pounding nails into his eyes and throat), he deliberately censors some information, mainly relating to sexuality, contained in the Italian manuscript. He is quite open about this self-censorship, using parenthetical material to alert his readers: "Here, it becomes absolutely impossible to follow the Roman narrator in the highly obscure relation of the strange things by which François sought to shock his contemporaries. His wife and his unfortunate daughter were, according to all evidence, victims of his abominable ideas" (*IC*, 1: 60). The Italian text is less chaste and specifies that Cenci put boys gathered in the street in his wife's bed and kept prostitutes in his palace. The same kind of censorship occurs later in relation to the execution of Béatrice's mother: "The details which follow are tolerable for the Italian public, which wants to know everything to the last detail; let it suffice for the French reader to know that this poor woman's chastity caused her to be wounded in the chest; the butcher showed the head to the people and then wrapped it in the black taffeta veil" (*IC*, 1: 81). The Italian text elaborates that her breasts were wounded and that, once cut, her head continued to agitate for some time. Shortly afterwards, in recounting Béatrice's execution, Stendhal suppresses without announcing that he is doing so the detail that as Béatrice's head was cut, her leg leapt upwards uncovering her body almost to her head. Although some of these details could not have been published in *La Revue des Deux Mondes* in any case, this censoring reminds us that while strong erotic drives are present in Stendhal's texts, his writings remain descriptively chaste.

Since love does not constitute the dominant force in the narrative, "Vittoria Accoramboni" and "Les Cenci" differ from the other Italian chronicles and from most of Stendhal's fiction. As Hans Boll-

Johansen has shown, plots such as these in which action is preponderant are very rare in Stendhal's fiction.[2] In those texts Stendhal conceived mainly on his own, the evolution of the characters' sentiments is essential, while these two tales in particular and the *Italian Chronicles* generally stress the train of events in which they are involved. In addition, these two stories contain features that will reoccur in the others and that are characteristic of detective novels: crimes, suspects, clues, and police investigations.[3]

In 1838 Stendhal published another story, "The Duchess of Palliano," that follows the Italian text less closely than the two previous ones. He had three different manuscript sources at his disposal and combined elements from them as well as material of his own invention. In his preface he stresses the idea, quite current at the time, that mores and hence morals are relative to time and place. What moral values can be found in this tale relate to the mastery over self – something for which Stendhal had a deep admiration. The Duchess, her husband, and her brother-in-law the Cardinal all show such mastery when each is separately put to death. The Cardinal, the narrator tells us, was superior to his brother "because he used fewer words; words are always a force which one seeks outside of oneself" (*IC*, 1: 117). When he learned of his condemnation to death "he made his confession; he recited the seven psalms of penance, then sat on a chair and said to the butcher: '*Do it*.' The executioner strangled him with a silk rope which broke. It took him two more attempts. The cardinal looked at the executioner without deigning to say a word" (*IC*, 1: 118). These texts remind us that impulsive energy is not the only ethical norm Stendhal admires; the ethic of self-control is equally important to him. In this case as in others, self-control is frequently expressed at the level of language. There is in Stendhal a silence that can be termed heroic, and laconism is frequently a sign of strength.

As in the other stories, the characters are left undeveloped. Even the Duchess, who gives her name to the story, remains in the background and has little influence on the action. Although this is a love story, the reader does not witness the growth of love between the two characters. The narrator simply states that love exists, and there is no attempt to probe the depths of the psychology of love as is the case in the novels (see Boll-Johansen, 428). The plot clearly stresses actions and events and, as in the previous chronicles, does not shy away from scenes of horror. In this story three characters are hung on ropes, the duke bites Marcel on the cheek, Palliano cuts off Diane's head, and the Duchess is strangled with a rope. The text seems bent on exterminating the characters one at a time – a procedure that operates in practically all of the *Chronicles*.

This story, like the others, is not without a political message, for it is a stinging commentary on the government of the popes. Even the occasional honest pope – Paul IV in this story – is unable to control the corruption in his administration. In these tales filled with phony trials, papal justice is represented as capricious and deriving from personal or political motivations. Publishing these texts was a political act, for they are reminders of the seamy political past of the Holy See, then threatened by the Carbonari.

The last and most substantial story Stendhal published based on the chronicles is "L'Abbesse de Castro" ("The Abbess of Castro"). It appeared in 1839 in two installments in *La Revue des Deux Mondes*. The concept of the Italian chronicle has now considerably evolved, for Stendhal draws from the Italian text but a small part – roughly one-sixth – of this tale. The Italian manuscript relates only the the affair between the abbess and the bishop and has nothing to say about the love between Hélène de Campireali, the abbess of the title, and Jules Branciforte, which provides the major thrust of the story. The result is a much longer narrative – it occupies nearly 100 pages in most editions – that is more attentive to situation and character development and has a different ending from the Italian manuscript.

The story involves Hélène, a young woman from a wealthy family who falls in love with Jules, the son of a now-deceased but once-prominent member of a private, illegal, armed group. Hélène's family is much opposed to this relationship, and, to make matters worse, Jules is obliged, while participating in maneuvers with the private army, to kill Hélène's brother in self-defense. At that point the family locks up Hélène in a convent (ironically named the convent of the Visitation), which Jules unsuccessfully attempts to take by storm. The leader of the outlaws then sends him off to fight in Spain. Hélène's mother sees to it that forged letters purporting to be from Jules and revealing the gradual waning of his love reach Hélène. After a while Hélène's mother falsifies the news that he has died. Hélène thereafter is seduced by the local bishop, by whom she has a child. This relationship is discovered, the bishop is jailed, and Hélène is confined to a dungeon room in another convent. Jules then returns to Italy. On learning that he is still alive, Hélène, filled with remorse at having betrayed him, commits suicide.

Since the death of the heroine is known from the beginning, the interest does not lie in what her ultimate fate will be but rather in the events that will bring that fate about. The narrator, who purports to be but a translator, frequently refers to the two manuscripts he claims to be using, sometimes using quotation marks to indicate direct quotation, sometimes pretending to skip over details of lesser interest. This clever subterfuge aimed at creating an air of authenticity for his story also permits Stendhal to adopt a proleptic mode to his storytelling as he drops hints of what is to come.

Although mostly of Stendhal's invention, the story has much in common with the other tales. As usual in these narratives, the times and the mores explain behavior. In a first chapter devoted exclusively to background, the narrator is careful to situate his story in a sociopolitical and historical context. The role of the bandits, he maintains, is one that has been glossed over by historians. His explanation of that role exalts their bravery and energy and reveals his own fascination for people who operate outside the mainstream of society. In the context of tyrannical regimes, the bandits emerge as a counter-power to governments, more as rebels than outlaws. This type of society, which the narrator is quick to contrast with French society, is one that produces great art and great passions. "In those days," he states almost nostalgically, "one saw passion" (*IC*, 1: 121).

Religion, which does not figure prominently in the background chapter, emerges in the story proper mainly as superstition (e.g., Jules says his rosary before attacking the convent), but it is nevertheless very important in this story in which piety and eroticism are conjoined. An example can be found in the episode in which Hélène, on the verge of yielding to Jules sexually, hears the sound of the "Ave Maria" and asks him to forgo their intimacy in honor of the Madonna. He readily agrees on condition that she swear on a Cross that she will be his whenever he asks her to – something he later reminds her of when he wants her to yield to him: "And you swore on this cross . . . and on your eternal damnation, that in whatever place you might be, and whatever might happen, the moment that I would give you the word, you would place yourself at my entire disposition, as you were at that very moment when the *Ave Maria* from

Mount Cavi reached your ears. Then we devoutly recited two *Aves* and two *Paters*" (*IC*, 1: 178). The very piety that had protected Hélène's virginity is now demanding that she yield to her lover. It is a peculiarity of Italian Catholicism, in Stendhal's depiction, that piety and morality do not interfere with each other. This is a Catholicism without moralism, without morality even, which contrasts sharply with the very moralistic Catholicism of the French Restoration.

The story's length allows for greater attention to character than is the case in the other Italian tales. Hélène is caught in the Cornelian dilemma of having to choose between competing allegiances – between fidelity to her lover and fidelity to her family. She is faithful to her lover, but her hesitations permit her mother's schemes to bring about her downfall. Having lost Jules, Hélène degenerates into a haughty, vain, and ambitious woman whose final act of suicide is an effort to redeem herself. Her mother, a strong and willful woman, is first presented as a sympathetic character who very much loves her daughter. After her son dies at Jules's hand, however, she emerges as cunning and ultimately malicious. This does not detract from her considerable ability to manage situations. The manner in which she negotiates with the Cardinal, for example, is quite admirable and recalls Duchess Sanseverina in *The Charterhouse of Parma*. Jules, who is in the foreground during the first five chapters, remains in the background during the last two. He is nevertheless a solidly delineated character who is very much a part of the society Stendhal was at pains to describe in the first chapter. He comes closer to the heroes of Stendhal's novels than does any other male protagonist in the Italian chronicles. Significantly, like the novelistic heroes, he judges himself, believing himself at one point to be but a fool. Even such minor characters as Jules's mentor, Fabrice Colonna, have an unusual consistency for secondary characters in Stendhal.

This tale differs from Stendhal's novels by its paucity of dialogue.[4] Communication is sometimes effected by things (a bouquet of flowers) or sounds (the "Ave Maria"). More frequently, it is done by the written word. The first communication between the lovers is a letter from Jules to Hélène; the last is a letter from Hélène to Jules. These two letters frame a text in which signs are shown to be dangerous. In considering a response to Jules's letter, Hélène "didn't know what sign she could permit herself" (*IC*, 1: 137). Indeed, the fear of revealing too much too directly is at the root of the problems between the lovers. They exchange notes and letters, yet when they communicate face to face, each holds back. When Hélène does talk it is to the wrong person – namely, her mother, who uses these confidences to further control her daughter. Trusting written communication, however, leaves open the possibility that it will be intercepted and destroyed, which is what Fabrice Colonna does to Jules's letters to Hélène. More seriously still, it allows for forgeries such as those concocted by Hélène's mother. The tragedy of this story, finally, is one of miscommunication. Indeed, the world of the *Italian Chronicles* is always one in which communication is difficult, if not impossible.

The claustration of the woman loved occupies the thematic center of this story in which immurement in a convent signals the inaccessibility and impossibility of love. The desired woman is surrounded by thick, black walls that, according to the narrator, make the convent look like a fortress. Sets of walls inside these walls form a kind of "Piranesian labyrinth"⁵ with metal locks, doors, and grills at every corner. Jules tries but cannot penetrate all these walls; only the bishop succeeds, but he is disdained by the woman he loves, and the relationship is judged illicit. There are other symbolic walls in this story, such as those that divide the Campirealis from the Brancifortis and the Colonnas from the Orsinis. In Stendhal's universe passionate love necessarily collides with obstacles.

There are several other uncompleted texts drawn from the Italian manuscripts, all containing a number of features common to the other tales. One of these, "Suora Scolastica," although it takes place in the eighteenth rather than the sixteenth century, bears a resemblance to "The Abbess of Castro," and its composition seems to have proceeded in the same manner. Stendhal took a brief Italian text about a woman in a convent being pursued by a lover on the outside and wrote a narrative that led to this situation. This story, on which he was working at the time of his death, reveals that he still had a mastery of good storytelling techniques, that he was still adept at depicting the body language of passion, and, especially, that he was still fascinated by the idea of a lover being held in a convent. Since Stendhal died before he could finish the story, it is uncertain how he would have ended it, and he seems to have been working with at least three possible endings. Another unfinished tale, also written the year of Stendhal's death, "Trop de faveur tue" (Too Much Favor

Kills), stays very close to the Italian original but once again shows Stendhal's interest in the subject of desire inside convent walls. In this case such confinement leads to murders and poisonings.

In all these tales the psychological forces are more static but the passions more violent and the sanctions against passion more severe than in the novels. In contrast to the novels, the *Chronicles* emphasize external plot, focusing on the characters' actions rather than their feelings and sentiments. Moreover, external time (signaled by the frequency of historical dates) takes precedence over internal time (Boll-Johansen, 430).

Chapter Seven

The Charterhouse of Parma:
The Masked Comedy

Among the manuscripts Stendhal had used to write the *Italian Chronicles*, one is of special importance. Entitled "Origins of the greatness of the Farnese family," it relates how Vannozza Farnese was able to promote her nephew Alexander's fortunes with the help of her powerful lover, Roderic, a cardinal who later became pope. Alexander was nevertheless imprisoned for having kidnapped a young woman, although he managed to escape and later became a cardinal. He continued his dissolute life until he fell in love with a young woman named Cleria, whom he treated as his wife and from whom he had numerous children. All of this remained a secret and, at age 67, Alexander became Pope Paul III. Stendhal saw in this tale the potential for a story similar to the other Italian chronicles he had composed and proceeded to write a rather liberal adaptation of it.

On 3 September 1838, however, he suddenly conceived the idea of transposing the story to the nineteenth century and expanding it into a novel. He worked two days on the project, stopped for an unknown reason, and began again on 4 November, working at tremendous speed, dictating parts of it to a transcriber, until 25 December when he had completed it. *La Chartreuse de Parme* (*The Charterhouse of Parma*) was thus written in seven weeks or, to be precise, 52 days. It is his most sustained depiction of Italy and the Italian character he so much admired. The transposition to the nineteenth century permits him to situate his story within the context of European politics after the Congress of Vienna while at the same time retaining the personal mores he associated with Renaissance Italy.

Politics

In each of his novels Stendhal feigns to include political material only reluctantly, claiming to do so solely because of the requirements of faithful representation. *The Charterhouse of Parma*, which also contains such a disclaimer, boldly begins with a major political and historical event – namely, Napoleon's entry into Milan in May 1796. The narrator is particularly keen on relating the impact of the event on the people of Milan. Whereas this once courageous people had become passive, effeminate subjects who printed sonnets on little handkerchiefs made of pink taffetas, after Napoleon's arrival this same people became energetic and "to risk one's life became fashionable" (*CP*, 1: 11). The effete mores, in the narrator's perspective, are connected with the political tyranny under which the Milanese had been living. Once they had overturned the statues of Charles V and Philip II, "all of a sudden, they were flooded with light" (*CP*, 1: 11). The youthfulness of the French soldiers bringing liberty is truly infectious, as the people of Milan cast off both their elders and their old ways. One of the purposes of these buoyant, initial pages, then, is to stress the cultural, social, and psychological effects of political freedom. Dictatorship entails a moral degeneration of its subjects, while freedom leads to moral greatness.

The initial pages also establish a gauge against which tyranny is to be measured, for the freedom of Milan is short-lived, and the remainder of the novel's action takes place under dictatorships – first in Milan under the tyranny of the Austrians and then, in Parma, under the petty tyranny of Ranuce-Ernest IV. While much of Stendhal's narrative of the goings-on in the latter regime is parodic, the political situation described by *The Charterhouse of Parma* nevertheless reveals the stresses and dangers of a repressive regime in which no one can feel secure against someone else's denunciation. In such a situation, the oppressed themselves become morally debased. For example, the inmates of the Farnese prison, who are kept in inhuman conditions, have a "Te Deum" sung when their cruel jailer, who is believed to be in danger of death, is revealed to be safe. Dictatorship skews the minds of men.

The ample caricature notwithstanding, the conditions described are not an invention of Stendhal's imagination, for repression was the order of the day in most of Europe in the aftermath of the

Napoleonic wars. Yet, one of the ironies of postrevolutionary repression is that those who are responsible for it are not masters in their own house. Ranuce-Ernest IV cannot rid himself of Count Mosca, whose skill and intelligence are essential to his desire to become king of all northern Italy and who, moreover, has documents that could embarrass Ranuce-Ernest. Nor can the prince control his notorious minister of justice, Rassi. Furious that Rassi has officially sent the sentence of Fabrice (the protagonist) to the governor of the Citadel, he threatens to have him tried and expelled. Rassi insolently defies him to do so, reminding him that there is no one else who is able to manipulate the justice system for the prince's ends as effectively as he. Knowing he need not fear the consequences of Ranuce-Ernest's displeasure, Rassi coolly informs Count Mosca of the prince's decision to have Fabrice poisoned.

Rassi's activities are so distasteful that Stendhal has recourse to farce as the only way to represent him. He is spoken to as to the lowest of servants by Mosca, and the prince treats him like a buffoon, slapping and kicking him in the manner of third-rate comedies. He is, nevertheless, a dangerous man; the basis of his power "lies in his ability to represent events as conspiracies" (Jefferson, 172). To make himself indispensable to the new prince, Ranuce-Ernest V, he wants to have some liberals hanged for poisoning the late prince. Were such an event to occur, terror would then reign and Rassi would be as necessary to Prince Ranuce-Ernest V as he had been to his father. The young prince finds himself in a position similar to Nero in Racine's play *Brittanicus*, who, at a crossroads in his life, had to decide between two opposing arguments – one leading to good, another to evil. Duchess Sanseverina's advice, similar to that given by Burrhus to Nero, is that he ignore Rassi's pleas if he wants a trouble-free reign. Unlike Nero, Ranuce-Ernest takes the good advice and does not have the liberals hanged.

Rassi's is but one type of possible political activity in an Italian city-state at this time. Another is open revolt, the option followed by Ferrante Palla. By profession a medical doctor, he is also, in the opinion of both the count and the duchess, the greatest poet in northern Italy. While he might be seen as a symbol of suppressed talent, he seems to enjoy the life he is leading. Others affirm that he is insane, and he certainly does act like a crazed man when he expresses his love for the duchess or when he proposes to give up his life for either the duchess or the freedom of Parma. The numerous analogies between his situation and that of Fabrice, however, would seem to indicate that both of them represent the madness of sublime love.[1] It is clear that in Stendhal's ethic, it is such fools who are sane. Still, Ferrante's revolt fails, thanks to the energetic action of Count Mosca, but perhaps also because he has little to offer as a leader other than a fanatical devotion to republican ideals.

The rebellion's repressor, Count Mosca, is an intelligent and witty man who has risen to the rank of prime minister by treating politics as a game to be played shrewdly. In this respect, he is the opposite of Gina's first husband, Count Pietranera, who, after Napoleon's fall, preferred to live in poverty rather than accept any political compromises. Yet during Ferrante's brief revolt (unwittingly financed by Duchess Sanseverina) against the regime, Mosca fires general P*** for having suggested negotiations with the rebels, takes personal command of the soldiers, and has 60 men shot for having attacked the prince's statue. If successful, the attack on the prince's statue would have been a symbolic victory over tyranny, even if the prince himself were not toppled. Ferrante and his fellow revolutionaries might have then accomplished in Parma at least temporarily what Napoleon's armies had achieved in Milan in 1796, when the statues of Charles V and Philip II were toppled.

Mosca explains that he would have given his life for the prince. Why, we are led to wonder, would a consummate political player do this? Certainly not to maintain his own power. He has many times wanted to resign and has remained in office only because the duchess insisted that he do so. Indeed, he will later resign. Nor does he do it out of loyalty to the prince, since he had already participated in Fabrice's escape – a treasonous act for a high government official. We know that he does not believe in the prince's politics, but his reaction to the revolt also confirms that he does not believe that Italy is ready for republicanism. He is not alone in this belief, for Ferrante Palla himself draws this conclusion in his farewell letter to the duchess. This might explain why Mosca puts down a rebellion that in his judgment would lead but to further chaos, bloodshed, and invasion by foreign powers. But there is surely another factor at play here – namely, Mosca's high sense of personal honor. For him, politics is but a game that he enjoys and that allows him to stray from government policy in dealing with Rassi and in trying to have Fabrice escape. But the moment that the prince's statue is attacked, his own honor is at stake, and he does his duty as prime minister. The "amoral" Mosca does live by an exacting code.

Mosca's boss, Ranuce-Ernest IV, could easily have been depicted as a monster, for he maintains a harsh prison, intimidates his subjects, relies on corrupt officials and judges, and is capable of personal cruelty. Stendhal treats him with intermittent humor, however, and seems more interested in the psychology behind political repression than he is in the realistic representation of a tyrant. Like all petty, post-Napoleonic despots, Ranuce-Ernest is a bored man, but he is a severe dictator primarily because he is afraid. Since he has had two liberals executed, he is now, according to Mosca, constantly subject to fears of all kinds. To mask these fears and give the impression of being self-assured, he imitates Louis XIV and Joseph II, although this activity also underscores the extent to which his politics is one of representation. While Stendhal condemns the regime, he does not entirely condemn him: "The prince was not an evil man, whatever the Italian liberals might say about him. It is true that he had a number of them thrown into prison, but it was out of fear" (*CP*, 1: 238). In the narrator's eyes, if the prince is worthy of contempt, it is not so much for the harshness of his rule as for his ridiculously anachronistic behavior.

It may appear perplexing that Stendhal, himself a notorious liberal, has chosen as his major characters supporters of a reactionary regime who consider their wealth and power due to them because of their birth. How do we explain that he would represent these characters rather positively, while depicting the liberals as villains? The driving force for liberalism is an unscrupulous, scheming, and unprincipled woman, Marquise Raversi, while the titular head of the liberal party is unrivaled as a cruel jailer. The only principled republican is a wild-eyed fanatic who would give up his politics for a duchess. Stendhal seems to be stating that political life, here as in *The Red and the Black*, is marked by incoherence, that ideologies are subject to change according to their proponents' relationship to power, and that political labels are not fixed. Gina and Mosca are both suspected of Jacobinism by the prince because of their intellectual freedom. Mosca has fought for Napoleon in Spain, and Gina's first husband was one of Napoleon's generals. On the other hand, Fabio Conti, who aspires to become the first liberal prime minister of

Parma, is the cruel governor of the reactionary government's prison. After the rebellion, Mosca's enemies charge *him* with being a liberal, and a new conservative party emerges led by Marquise Raversi and Rassi. Raversi and Rassi no doubt feel they are close to power.

In Stendhal's readings of the politics of nineteenth-century Europe, conservatives become liberals when out of power (Monsieur de Rênal in *The Red and the Black*), and liberals become conservatives when in power (the government of Louis-Philippe in *Lucien Leuwen*). Both labels mask a similar quest for power that is more important to its aspirants than ideology. Neither is a real threat to the existing regime, as the prince, who is capable of occasional political insight, recognizes.

Faced with such complexity and incoherence, Gina and Mosca profess the ideals of libertarian aristocracy. Conscious of the perils of both monarchic despotism and tyranny by the majority, they are partisans of moral and intellectual freedom. Reactionary in their anti-egalitarianism, they are liberal in their love of personal liberty.[2] It is precisely the aristocratic tradition's libertarian element that Stendhal admires in these aristocrats who are not to be confused – not morally, intellectually, or politically – with the historical aristocracy. For Stendhal, whose cynicism toward politics and political systems only grew with time, intellectual and moral freedom emerge as ideals to which an individual can aspire under any regime. Freedom of thought and action is his private answer to the inability of politics to provide for authentic public freedom.

A Young Man's Quest

Although Fabrice del Dongo differs from Stendhal's other protagonists by being archetypally marked as a hero,[3] he is, like Stendhal's other heroes, a young man in the process of becoming an adult. For Fabrice, the passage from adolescence into adulthood involves a process of disillusion that begins with his attempt to join Napoleon's armies. Before his presence at the battle of Waterloo, he had seen war as an outlet for high sentiments such as honor, duty, valor, and generosity. Now that he has become engaged in an actual war, he is totally disillusioned:

> He could not console himself of such infamy, and his back leaning against a willow, he began weeping profusely. One at a time, his dreams were unravelling, all those beautiful dreams of chivalrous and sublime friendship, like those of the heroes of *Jerusalem Delivered*. Seeing death approach was nothing, when you were surrounded by tender and heroic souls, by noble friends who clasp your hand at the moment of your last breath! But to retain your enthusiasm surrounded by such vile scoundrels!!! (*CP*, 1: 98)

Later, when he tries to buy a piece of bread from his comrades, they answer with sarcasm and laughter, much to his astonishment: "So war was not that noble and mutual uplifting of souls taken with glory that he had imagined from Napoleon's proclamations!" (*CP*, 1: 99). Shortly thereafter, when Corporal Aubry explains to Fabrice that everyone is a traitor in this war, "the scales fell from Fabrice's eyes" (*CP*, 1: 118). Like Don Quixote before him and Madame Bovary after him, Fabrice had believed in the truth of texts. The time it takes for him to come to terms with reality underscores the quixotic nature of his imaginings. Victor Brombert has pertinently remarked that in his manner of relating Fabrice's disillusion, Stendhal is debunking the notion of the epic hero as well (Brombert, 155).

The Waterloo episode translates its author's desire to divest war of its romantic and heroic trappings. Stendhal has chosen to depict a defeat, with fleeing soldiers who, far from being heroic and noble, are ready to kill for a horse. It is noteworthy that in narrating this episode Stendhal allows himself some of the few instances of realistic detail in his fiction. He describes a corpse with one eye open in which a bullet had entered next to the nose and had exited by the opposite temple thereby horribly disfiguring the face; a wounded horse that in struggling was cutting his own sides with his hoofs; and a soldier having his leg cut. These rare forays into descriptive realism have as their purpose to depict war as an ugly, bloody business, quite the opposite of a noble and glorious adventure.

The description of the battle of Waterloo highlights the type of realism – based on the point of view of one individual – which Stendhal used in his other novels. In contrast to Victor Hugo, whose description of the same battle in his *Les Misérables* involves a grand-scale depiction of the engagement, Stendhal's battle is notable for its incoherence. Since he cannot see the whole, Fabrice is even unsure whether it is a battle or not, and he never does find out whether it was the battle of Waterloo. The reader shares the same sense of disconnectedness, for he too sees only what Fabrice sees. For Stendhal, who had himself witnessed combat, this presentation was closer to the truth: no individual soldier can experience the totality of such an event. The originality of this presentation of war was clear to Tolstoy, who acknowledged his own debt to it.

Although Fabrice is disillusioned about war, he does not appear to mature from the experience – nor, for that matter, does he mature from any of his other adventures in the first half of the novel. Rather than reflect and possibly grow from experience, he seems compelled to put on one disguise after another. More than any other of Stendhal's characters, Fabrice is forced to play roles, to wear masks. At various points in the first third of the novel he claims to be a barometer merchant, a captain of the fourth regiment of hussars, a young bourgeois in love with the wife of the captain of the fourth regiment of hussars, someone named Teulier, then Boulot, then Cavi, then Ascagne Pietranera, and, finally, an unnamed peasant. In the first seven chapters Fabrice has used at least eight different names or disguises. And that is not the end of it. He will disguise himself to go to Marietta's apartment, use Giletti's name and passport to go through customs, after which we see him disguised as a rich rural bourgeois. He then pretends to be Ludovic's brother and, a few pages later, a theology student named Joseph Bossi. During the Fausta episode he passes himself off as the valet of a great English lord. When he duels with Count M***, he calls himself Bombace.

Why all these roles? Unlike Julien Sorel, Fabrice is not driven to adopt personas out of a need to conceal his true thoughts. The masks are necessary as a protection against others (governments and individuals) who would clearly do him harm, were they to know who he really is.

All Stendhal's heroes feel a need to protect the self – a need the author seems to have shared. Indeed, all his male characters wear masks and change or would want to change their names. None of the previous heroes, however, are ever in any real danger. But there may be a more significant difference. Ann Jefferson has appropriately pointed out that a number of Fabrice's masks were chosen for him by others (Jefferson, 194) in an effort to help him avoid detection. Most of those he chose for himself were for the purpose of seeing a loved one undetected. Jefferson's point is crucial: Fabrice never disguises himself to fool people he loves.

The ease with which he accepts the masks provided by others and the similar ease with which he dons his own masks do not detract from his strong sense of *who* he is – namely, a Del Dongo. Being a Del Dongo identifies his genealogy and class and allows him various privileges and rights which he does not question. Ironically, there is every reason to believe that he is not really a Del Dongo. Stendhal informs his readers that Fabrice "happened to be, by accident of birth, the second son of that Marquis del Dongo, so great a nobleman" (*CP*, 1: 26). Various indications in the text lead us to surmise, however, that his father was a French lieutenant named Robert who was lodged at their residence in Milan during the French occupation and who was quite taken by the Marquise del Dongo's beauty. Her husband spent little time at his Milan residence in that period, and Fabrice was born one year after Robert's arrival. Later, Fabrice's mother, who maintains a correspondence with Robert, worries about what he might think of Fabrice's education (or, rather, lack thereof), thereby suggesting that he might have some interest in what becomes of Fabrice. In his revisions for a projected new edition of *The Charterhouse of Parma*, Stendhal has Canon Borda recall a rumor that Fabrice was the son of Lieutenant Robert.

Yet Fabrice's strong sense of being a Del Dongo, however mistaken, does not tell him what kind of person he really is. This is, for much of the novel, an open question. At first he thinks he is a soldier, but then he becomes a member of the clergy, not out of a sense that this is his vocation but because others have proposed this course to him. While Fabrice does not search for his essence with the same intensity as Lucien Leuwen, he does clearly want to know what he is. He is constantly asking everyone if what he just witnessed was a battle because he wants to know if he is a hero. Masks, in addition to the protection they afford the individual who is threatened from the exterior, also signal a character in search of himself. This reading concurs with the fundamental themes of *Lucien Leuwen* and *Life of Henry Brulard*, both written in the same period.

In contrast to Balzac, whose characters are often the incarnation of an abstraction, Stendhal creates characters whose essence is not established until very late in the novel. Indeed, Balzac, who had a very high opinion of *The Charterhouse of Parma*, criticized it on this very point. For him, Fabrice is much too elusive and far overshadowed by his aunt and her lover. If Fabrice was to be the main character, the novel should have been renamed, in Balzac's judgment, *Fabrice; or, The Nineteenth-Century Italian*. That is, Balzac would have wanted Fabrice to be a *type*, a representative "of the young Italians of today."[4] But this is precisely what Stendhal wishes to avoid. His refusal to make of his protagonists types is what led Victor Brombert to propose that a century before Malraux, Stendhal had proclaimed that men are what they make themselves (Brombert, 174). Yet for some of Stendhal's characters, such as Julien and Fabrice, their acts contribute to their essence in a negative way only. Both characters come to realize that their previous activities were not of much value but that love and intimacy are. The important point here is that the narrator does not endow them with an essence from the beginning but allows them to discover themselves.

Aside from his difficulties with the law, Fabrice has another problem that, for him, is more fundamental: he thinks he is incapable of falling in love. The text makes it clear that he has no physical impediments. He is capable of having sex, but he knows that is not love: "I have feelings of love just as I am hungry at six o'clock! Could it be this rather vulgar propensity that those liars have turned into the love of Othello, the love of Tancrede?" (*CP*, 1:362). Some time later, he exclaims, "I'm incapable of rising above vulgar pleasure" (*CP*, 1:383). On many occasions he expresses his incapacity to love: "It is love that is wanting in me" (*CP*, 1:267); "the passion [of love] is foreign to [my] heart" (*CP*, 1:277); "my soul is not susceptible to love" (*CP*, 1:377). By this he means that he cannot feel love in the way he believes that love should be experienced. When he speaks of the women he has courted in Naples or elsewhere, he recalls that he never thought of them when they were not present. For him, love should totally take over the person who is in love. He does not quite know what love is, but he knows that it is not only sensual, that it is a noble experience that has both emotional and intellectual elements.

It is in this context that his feelings toward the duchess are best addressed. Duchess Sanseverina, who has other names and titles and is frequently referred to as Gina, is so powerful a character that she comes close to becoming the novel's chief protagonist. In a preliminary note to the reader, Stendhal implies that this is the story of the duchess, and, indeed, for the first third of the novel it is not clear whether this novel is about Fabrice or Gina. One critic was so taken up with this character as to call her "one of the most glamorous and vital women of modern fiction."[5] She is, to be sure, a woman of extraordinary strength of character. Endowed with wit and intelligence and spontaneous, resourceful, and oblivious to convention, she has a flair for theatrics and is capable of cruelty and even vengeance. Her love for Fabrice grows into something that is more than auntly, although it takes a long time for her to admit this to herself. Both she and Fabrice are held back by the incest taboo, although Gina, as the sister of the Marquis del Dongo, who very well may not be Fabrice's father, may not be his aunt. More important than these real or apparent relations is the fact that Gina in many ways functions as a second mother for Fabrice. She passes him off as her son on one occasion early in the novel, and Mosca says of her later that "she has loved him like a son for fifteen years" (*CP*, 1: 259). In pleading with Ranuce-Ernest V for Fabrice's life, she admits to "being overwhelmed by the foolish fears of the soul of a mother" (*CP*, 2: 291).

Gina's love for him does make Fabrice uncomfortable. He knows that she will never speak of it because she would be horrified at the thought of incest. What he fears is that in some moment of folly she might say something that would require him to react. This happens later when he proposes to go to Sanguina to supervise Count Mosca's archaeological digs. The duchess, overcome with emotion, throws herself into his arms and says, "So, you want to run away from me," forcing him to answer, "No, but I would like to be prudent" (*CP*, 1: 132). In truth, much of what Fabrice does is explained in part by the necessity to flee his aunt's love. Ironically, he who refuses incest will end up in a jail originally built to house a crown prince guilty of incest.

In any case, Fabrice does not feel for his aunt what he believes he should feel were he in love. He has, to be sure, tried to find ideal love, having gone to much trouble to gain La Fausta's affections, but he has not experienced the emotional satisfaction he seeks. Soon after the La Fausta episode, however, he encounters Clélia, who is different from any other woman he has ever met. An angelic beauty with a nobility of soul that resembles that of Armance and Madame de Chasteller, she is clearly the answer to his quest. Bringing such a love to fruition, however, requires overcoming numerous difficulties related to circumstance (she is the jailer's daughter), physical impossibility (he is locked in a cell), religious impediments (he is a member of the clergy), and, most importantly, her own character.

She had never wanted to marry because she wanted to protect her interior life: "She was stricken by a kind of horror at the very thought of placing the solitude that was so dear to her as well as her intimate thoughts at the disposition of a young man whose role as husband would authorize him to trouble her entire interior life" (*CP*, 2: 42). When she falls in love with Fabrice, her own words and actions are limited by her fear of losing or not meriting Fabrice's esteem. What disturbs her, for example, after having been unable to respond to one of his questions, is that he "will have seen in [her] a base person. . . . This idea brought despair to this young woman who had such a noble soul" (*CP*, 2: 37). Since she is without a mother or even a female friend in whom to confide, her anguishing decisions must be made in solitude. This explains, in part, the role that religion plays in her life. Because she has no one from whom she can seek counsel, she relies on religion and particularly on the Madonna. The result is a morality based on a personal contract with the Madonna that will impair her relationship with Fabrice. That in Stendhal's universe love is always greater for overcoming the interdictions of religion does not make Clélia's and Fabrice's relationship any easier.

Important changes occur in Fabrice because of his love for Clélia. He who previously had always been fleeing the "eyes" of others, who always considered it necessary to be disguised in order not to be seen, now wants to be seen. True love has cured Fabrice of his fear of others. Significantly, this love grows despite great difficulties in communication between the lovers, who must resort to eye language, flashing letters of the alphabet, and pretending to address a third party. Fabrice's being in love with Clélia will also resolve at least partially the doubts about himself that have tormented him since adolescence. The fact that he now knows he is capable of passionate love will render unimportant such questions as whether or not he had been present at the battle of Waterloo. Now that he is in love, Fabrice comes to understand that what he is, whether or not he is a hero, for example, is of no importance. Love, especially when combined with isolation, leads not so much to self-knowledge as to a realization that self-knowledge is not important. No longer will Fabrice ask himself if he is a hero.

Within this context the thematics of heights reveals its special importance. Heights are symbols of moral elevation for Stendhal, representing moments when the hero finds himself above the crowd, both morally and physically. In *The Red and the Black* Julien leads a frenetic life, except when he is able to spend a few moments in the mountains near Verrières. He regains this calm only at the end of the novel, when, imprisoned, he is placed in a cell on an upper floor. In *The Charterhouse of Parma* this motif first occurs when Fabrice is in Abbé Blanès's tower. The narrator recounts that "that day spent imprisoned in a belfry was perhaps one of the happiest of his life" (*CP*, 1: 288-89). Since the other such elevated place is the prison tower at the Farnese prison, the motif of heights fuses with that of prisons – a literary motif with which Stendhal, through his readings of Cellini, Pellico, and others, was quite familiar.

In *The Red and the Black* the elevated place in which Julien finds himself at the end of the novel is, precisely, a prison. Like the mountain and Abbé Blanès's tower, prison provides isolation from others. Once in prison, Fabrice becomes happy almost spontaneously and without knowing why. The narrator writes that "strangely and without reflection, a secret joy reigned in the depths of his soul" (*CP*, 2: 100). A bit later Fabrice is astonished by the fact that although he is in prison he is not at all unhappy: "What? I need to think about it in order to be distressed in this prison? . . . In any case, it is certainly astonishing to be in prison and to have to think of reasons to be unhappy" (*CP*, 2: 103-4). At first, reading himself as a character of literature or history, he thinks that his happiness might indicate that he has a great soul, that he is a hero. But then he realizes that it is Clélia's presence that accounts for his mood. Love, not literature, is the reality. Herein lies the paradox of the happy prison.

At one point or another practically all of Stendhal's heroes seek a withdrawal from society. Even a character as little inclined to solitude as is Duchess Sanseverina was sensitive to the freedom of the Farnese tower. Before Fabrice's imprisonment she had, on a day when the heat in Parma was stifling, climbed to the top of the tower where "in that elevated position, she found air, which so delighted her that she spent several hours there" (*CP*, 1: 214). Heights permit one to breathe. In the case of the duchess, it is relief from the heat of Parma. But the stifling heat of Parma is also a metaphor for a stifling atmosphere from which Clélia will also seek refuge, also in an iso-

lated tower. Some time later it is Parma, with its political and social
life, that appears to Fabrice as a place of exile: "and you would like
me to do something as stupid as to exile myself to Parma" (*CP*,
2: 148). And then, "Has anyone ever escaped from a place where he
is at the height of happiness to go into an awful exile where everything is lacking, even the air to breathe?" (*CP*, 2: 162). We would
normally expect that it would be in prison that air would be lacking,
but for Fabrice it is precisely in Parma where one suffocates and in
prison that one can breathe.

While reflecting on Fabrice in the Farnese tower, it is instructive
to recall Fabrice's joyful day spent in Abbé Blanès's belfry, for this
earlier experience anticipates his stay in the Farnese prison. Stephen
Gilman has written of a convergence of the past, present, and future
during this episode.[6] What Fabrice sees from this tower recalls various things from his own past: birds that must be the descendants of
birds he had tamed some years earlier; adolescent girls he had
known as little girls. Yet more important than this link with the past
is the link with the future, for a number of similarities exist between
Fabrice's stay in Blanès's tower (twice referred to metaphorically as a
prison) and his stay in the Farnese prison. Both are towers from
which the Alps are visible, both have orange trees nearby, and the
birds Fabrice sees from the observatory reappear as Clélia's birds. In
the Farnese tower Fabrice is placed in a kind of wooden cage – a
description also used for Blanès's observatory – and in both towers
he is awakened suddenly. Finally, in prison, Fabrice makes a hole in
the louvers to see out, just as in Blanès's tower he had placed a cloth
in front of him and then had made holes in it for him to see.

Many events in *The Charterhouse of Parma* repeat themselves
with variants. Indeed, the prophecies alluded to and actually pronounced have meaning only within a structure of narrative repetition. This has led C. W. Thompson to propose that repetition might
be the novel's organizing principle.[7] Repetition, including prophecy,
implies that there are limits to human freedom. In *The Red and the
Black* but especially in *The Charterhouse of Parma*, we seem to
enter a world invested with a secret structure or order, though this
need not imply fatalism. Abbé Blanès's predictions allow room for
Fabrice's freedom of choice ("If you resist the temptation to violence"). Fabrice's drama is played out in the context of a destiny that
leaves some room for maneuver. Such a context also makes it easier

to accept the vagaries of fate and hence, paradoxically, to live in the present.

By highlighting these coincidences between Fabrice's stay in Abbé Blanès's tower and his stay in prison, Stendhal is preparing Fabrice (and his readers as well) for the realization that separation from society is a protection for the self. Isolation is a response to the political problem raised at the outset of this chapter, and the prison therefore emerges as doubly symbolic. While prison clearly represents the limitations that society imposes on life, it is also symbolic of a liberation from the fixation of society. Fabrice realizes that his captivity is also his salvation. Freed, psychologically, from the annihilating gaze of others and his heart filled with love, the prison becomes the locus of his freedom.

Here it might be useful to inquire why Stendhal titled this novel *The Charterhouse of Parma* when this charterhouse is mentioned only twice and only once by its complete name. All we know about this monastery is that Fabrice retired there, lived a year there, and died there. His relationship to the charterhouse is, however, greater than might first seem the case. Herbert Morris has pointed out some interesting similarities between Fabrice's life in the prison and that of the monks in a charterhouse, a type of monastery founded by Saint Bruno in the eleventh century.[8] Like the monks, Fabrice discovers in the solitude of his cell that which had escaped him in society – that is, a psychological and metaphysical freedom, happiness, and love (for Fabrice the love of Clélia replaces the love of God). Fabrice writes in the margins of his breviary about his ecstasies of divine love as would a Carthusian: "He had written daily in the margins a very detailed diary of everything that was happening to him in prison; the great events were nothing else but the great ecstasies of *divine love* (this word divine replaced another which he did not dare write)" (*CP*, 2: 218). Just as Carthusians are not allowed to speak, so also it is forbidden for Fabrice to speak or even for anyone else to talk to him. He is allowed some fresh air every Thursday, just as the Carthusians were permitted to take a walk and speak once a week. Fabrice is authorized to take a walk at dusk, but that is precisely labeled an exception. The Carthusians also fast each Friday and on special feasts as Fabrice is required to do. And the hole Fabrice makes in the louvers of his window recalls the small window through which the Carthusians transmit their messages. Stendhal had at first wanted to call his novel *The Black Charterhouse*. If we accept that the prison is a symbolic charterhouse, then "the black charterhouse" could refer to the prison, which contains, incidentally, a black chapel (see Morris, 12-19).

The theme of freedom through imprisonment and isolation is all the more evident if we consider that if Abbé Blanès's tower foreshadows the Farnese prison, the prison, in turn, foreshadows the charterhouse and thereby Fabrice's final retreat. The title, then, relates to a fundamental theme of the novel. Certainly Stendhal does not propose the monastery as a practical solution, but Fabrice's final retreat stresses his understanding of the problem of the individual versus the other. Stendhal, whose characters are the happiest when they can see without being seen, anticipates Sartre's contention in *Huis Clos* – that it is the stare of other people that constitutes our hell. Fabrice's retreat is in part a poetic affirmation of the value of isolation from that stare.

Though he shares many traits with Stendhal's other heroes, Fabrice emerges as fundamentally different in one significant way. An important text in this respect is Fabrice's own words: "I'm always comparing myself to a perfect model that cannot exist. Well! I forgive myself for my fear" (*CP*, 1: 295). As Shoshana Felman has pointed out, Fabrice is the first Stendhalian hero who does not see himself as inferior, who does not feel himself to be a lesser person because of his shortcomings. Since he does not share the inferiority complex of the other heroes, he does not share their aspirations to superiority either. By forgiving his shortcomings, Fabrice is exorcizing the obsession with the ideal model that had haunted Stendhal's previous heroes. This is what has permitted Felman to propose that Octave, Julien, and Lucien's existence are failed attempts to change themselves, to rewrite themselves in a way that approaches more completely an ideal model: "Fabrice does not seek to rewrite himself. On the contrary, only he learns to read himself" (Felman, 203). To be sure, his unique status among Stendhal's characters does not confer on him sound judgment. His insistence on fulfilling what he recognizes as a need – raising his own son – leads not only to his son's death but indirectly to his own and that of the two women who loved him. But he accepts the distance between himself and the ideal model as inherent to the human condition and forgives himself for being a man – the first of Stendhal's heroes to do so.

Closure

After the death of Fabrice's son, Sandrino, three short paragraphs bring the novel to a quick ending. Clélia dies, then Fabrice, then the duchess. These deaths, however, leave an opening for a possible continuity of which it is not for the reader to know. Fabrice, we are told, "hoped to rejoin Clélia in a better world" (*CP*, 2:372). The story of sublime love proposes to continue beyond the text. The novel ends with the sentence "The prisons of Parma were empty, the Count exceedingly rich, Ernest V adored by his subjects who compared his government to that of the grand dukes of Tuscany" (*CP*, 2:373). While one might read this sentence as a stylized closure in the manner of fairy tales, Victor Brombert has suggested that the phrase "the prisons of Parma were empty" could refer to a vanished happiness: the two prisoners of love, Fabrice and Clélia, are no more. Mosca's wealth certainly does not signal his happiness, since he has never put much stock in money and has now lost what he treasured the most – namely, Gina.[9]

Still, however, we appear to be witnessing a regime that has been greatly transformed. From a state with a feared ruler and full prisons, Parma now has empty prisons and a prince adored by his subjects. There is no reason in the text, however, to explain Ranuce-Ernest V's popularity with his people, and such a situation is at odds with the political situation in Parma that the narrator has described previously. Could it be that Mosca, now freed from love and jealousy, has channeled his considerable political skills to accomplish a political miracle? Given what we know about Stendhal's extreme skepticism regarding governments, we might wish to read this last sentence ironically. At the very least, this muted closure stands in sad contrast to the novel's exuberant opening. Philippe Berthier has aptly suggested that perhaps this last sentence, which is not at all necessary to complete the plot, is there to affirm that if the text stops, life continues – but it is a life unworthy of being put into a text.[10] A novel begun in exhilaration ends in resignation.

Chapter Eight

Lamiel: The Poetics of Energy

Lamiel, which was not available in print until 1889, was one of the last of Stendhal's writings to be published. It was written in 1839-40, with some revisions added up to the time of Stendhal's death in 1842. What is available to readers is a first version of an incomplete story, a revised version of the first part of this story (up to Lamiel's departure from the Château de Miossens), plus a series of sometimes disconnected fragments. This novel, the only one of Stendhal's not to be inspired by another text, is therefore in a much more primitive state than is *Lucien Leuwen*, which can be considered as nearly finished. It appears from these drafts that Stendhal was possibly anticipating making substantial changes later on. He died before he could put together a final copy, however.

The Continuing Chronicle

In addition to being the stories of individuals, Stendhal's novels are also chronicles of these people's times. From *Armance* through *Lucien Leuwen* his narratives reconstruct a composite picture of France during a relatively short period, roughly between 1827 and 1832. *Lamiel* was to be no exception to this chronicling impulse. Indeed, as he worked on the manuscript, particularly on the second and subsequent versions, Stendhal sought to broaden the scope of the novel. He even considered changing its title to *Les Français du Roi Philippe* (*The French of King Philip*), a clear indication that he was moving toward a broad description of French society under the July Monarchy, headed by King Louis-Philippe.

While politics may not be as important in *Lamiel* as it is in Stendhal's major novels, its role is not negligible. Indeed, a major political event, the revolution of 1830, serves as a reference point for the first half of the novel (particularly in the second version). The narrator is clearly intent on depicting how the aristocrats of Carville live in expectation of the revolution, "dying of fear and speaking every day of the return of a second Robespierre" (*L*, 14). So afraid are they of an imminent insurrection that when the village beadle unexpectedly arrives at the Château at eight o'clock in the evening, the Duchess de Miossens assumes that a revolution has taken place and that her son has been killed. These upper-Norman aristocrats were not entirely wrong in their fears. In the years preceding the revolution of 1830, nearby Rouen was considered a bastion of liberalism, a fact of which the duchess is very much aware: "Rouen is on its way to fire and blood like Paris; I won't be able to flee to Rouen; it's at Le Havre that I'll have to seek asylum" (*L*, 285-86). In her flight toward Le Havre with the intention of continuing on to England if circumstances require, the duchess thinks she is repeating the reaction of the nobility in 1789. This only highlights how super-annuated are her political ideas, for in 1830 most of the nobility offered no resistance at all; they simply withdrew from politics.

One of the duchess's functions in the novel is to represent an ignorant, bored, and fearful upper nobility that is the object of Stendhal's irony. She is one of the aristocrats who returned to France only in 1814 – something she considers a mark of distinction. Obsessed by rank and hierarchy, she has spent most of her life waiting for her father-in-law to die in order to become a duchess. So reactionary is she that she regards Louis XVIII as an "infamous Jacobin" (*L*, 177). She has, indeed, lost all contact with reality. In 1830 she still speaks of her "seigniorial rights" (*L*, 191), considers Voltaire and the Revolution as having never occurred, and continues to refer to the mayor of Carville as Monsieur l'Echevin – that is, by a title not used since the Revolution. Rejecting the dynamism of history, she has created a kind of feudal fantasy for herself, constructing a medieval tower on her property and artificially sustaining feudal customs such as the presentation of blessed bread. For her, as for the Marquis Del Dongo in *The Charterhouse of Parma*, history is static. What saves her as a character is the genuine affection she develops for Lamiel. Although a woman of strict formality, she is truly attracted by Lamiel's natural energy and seems to experience vicariously her spontaneity. Even the sardonic narrator is obliged to conclude that "deep down, she was a good soul" (*L*, 235) – a remark referring to her affection for Lamiel, however, not to her politics.

The duchess's son Fédor (called Hector or César in the first version) is handsome and refined, but above all weak. In the first version he is said to have left the Polytechnical School after the revolution of 1830 in order not to have to wear the tricolor cockade, an indication that he refuses to accept the results of the revolution and a sign that he is someone who can make a political choice. In the second, more definitive version, however, he is incapable of choosing between the Polytechnical School's liberalism and his mother's ancien régime mentality, giving credence to the narrator's remark in the first version that he lacked a strong will (*L*, 71). Yet he is genuinely in love with Lamiel, is utterly devoted to her, and shows considerable resourcefulness on her behalf. She, however, rejects this committed lover because, in her judgment, he lacks energy. Both the mother and the son attach themselves to Lamiel, who is of a lower social status, implicitly recognizing that the spontaneity she represents and that attracts them to her cannot be found in their own class.

Politically ineffective, these nobles oppose the 1830 revolution but do nothing to prevent or stop it, sealing their irrelevance. Not unexpectedly, the revolution shifts political power to the bourgeoisie and, in the Carville area in particular, to the cynical bourgeois doctor Sansfin. Although in one late version he reacts with fear when he learns of the revolution, the doctor, a reputed Jacobin, is willing to use the connections he has cultivated with the Congregation to advance his own ends. As a result, he is named subprefect in the Vendée (in another version he becomes a member of Parliament). By 1841 Stendhal was contemplating increasing Sansfin's role and broadening the novel's sociopolitical scope. There can be no doubt that *Lamiel*, as his final political statement, retains fully the sense of political cynicism manifested in his earlier novels.

Stendhal's cynicism regarding religion has, if anything, increased. Religion is a factor in all Stendhal's works, but in none of his novels does it come under as harsh an attack as it does in *Lamiel*, in which it is presented as a hoax. The incident that underlines the fraudulent character of religion is the phony miracle that occupies a prominent place early in the novel. To stimulate fear and belief in the Congregation, a missionary preacher, addressing an overflow crowd of faithful at dusk, arranges for an explosion of firecrackers from behind the altar at an appropriately threatening moment in a fire-and-brimstone sermon. He obtains the expected results: great fear, high emotion, faintings, and murmurs of a miracle. Even the beadle Hautemare, who had participated in setting up this hoax, is moved by it. Stendhal's approach to religion has clearly hardened. In *The Red and the Black* and *The Charterhouse of Parma* there had been an effort to balance an anticlerical discourse with positive clerical characters such as Abbé Chélan, Abbé Pirard, and Abbé Blanès. This novel makes no attempt to maintain such an equilibrium. Young Abbé Clément, to whom Stendhal does give positive traits, is too weak and fearful a character to play such a role.

If the Duchess de Miossens embodies the fatuities of the aristocracy, the Hautemares represent the stupidities of religion. They adopt Lamiel because Madame Hautemare, who had fainted from fear during the phony miracle, is moved to please God in this fashion (as well as to assure that there will be someone to care for her and her husband in their old age). This couple, for whom inadvertently eating soup containing some bouillon with fat in it on a Friday constitutes a moral crisis of the highest proportions, is incapable of distinguishing gradations of evil and "found sin in the least distraction" (*L*, 26). They consider such activities as reading books not meant for edification and dancing or even observing a dance as evils. While the sincerity of their beliefs is not challenged, the reader is also aware that their strict and open observance of the Church's rules has benefited them considerably. Hautemare has been rewarded by Abbé Du Saillard with a number of parish offices that have placed him in an economic situation superior to that of his peers.

Carville's pastor, Abbé Du Saillard (called Abbé Flamand in the first version) and the missionary priest, Abbé Le Cloud, are caricatures of narrow-minded, reactionary clerics. In contrast, Abbé Clément, who is pastor of a nearby village, is an intelligent, sensitive, and caring man. Like Fabrice, he continues, while falling in love, to preach faithfully the doctrines of the Church. Yet he differs from Fabrice in an essential way: he is unable to overcome the moral impediments to his love for Lamiel. In the first version the narrator specifies in the initial paragraph dealing with Abbé Clément that "without being aware of it, he fell in love with Lamiel" (*L*, 43). Later, when he chances to meet Lamiel in Paris, he realizes that she could be his: "With the open heart and the affection which she is showing towards me, I would only have to say a word" (*L*, 151). If faith and ethics are not related for the young Italian priest Fabrice, they are intimately connected in the mind of the young French priest Clément. This becomes very clear when Lamiel asks him to explain to her what love is. Forbidden by the moral code to which he adheres from verbalizing his love for Lamiel, he has recourse, uncharacteristically and not without embarrassment, to set formulas before having to flee Lamiel altogether. Later, when she comes to him for advice, he refuses to see her. However strong his feelings for Lamiel, he cannot overcome the impediments of a morality driven by Church rules.

This is a society, then, that is both politicized and highly moralistic. It is subject to the strong influence of the Church and peopled with individuals bound to convention. It is in such a setting that Stendhal places a young woman who is apolitical, amoral, antireligious, and unconventional. Her story is a biting commentary on that world.

The Education of a Young Woman

The second version of the first part of the novel (usually printed first in most editions since, as a later revision, it is seen as more definitive) opens, as does *The Red and the Black*, with a narrator who is a traveler. As the author of books on tourism, Stendhal was comfortable with this type of writing, and it is no surprise that the description of the Norman countryside in *Lamiel* replicates to a certain extent that which is found in *Memoirs of a Tourist* (1838). In addition to being a storyteller, this narrator, who is traveling from Paris to Carville, is a promoter of Normandy, which he touts as being as interesting as Switzerland without the hassle of a long trip and customs. In his enthusiasm he stresses the greenness and the variety of the countryside, which he sees as a kind of liberation "from the symmetries of Paris and its white walls" (*L*, 169). Once he reaches Carville, however, he does not find the liberation he anticipated. Although he enjoys hunting in the area, Carville itself turns out to be a dull, backward town, and he is obliged to spend boring evenings at the duchess's.

A change of place, which promises liberation, leads, then, to deception. As Leanne Wierenga has shown, this initial voyage prefigures a series of deceptions for Lamiel herself.[1] Her move from the orphanage to the Hautemares' home, from the Hautemares' to the Château, from Carville to Rouen, and from Rouen to Paris are all supposed to provide a liberation of some kind. Yet all these moves lead only to deception. The narrator's remark in the first version regarding her arrival at the Château, that "everything seemed magnificent, but after only three days of astonishment, she felt unhappy" (*L*, 34), could refer to each of Lamiel's moves. As Lamiel says, "It's necessary to beware of hope" (*L*, 63).

As an adolescent in the process of becoming an adult, Lamiel resembles Stendhal's other heroes. Once again we have a novel of formation, but in this case the protagonist is female. Dennis Porter has pointed out that the passage of a girl through adolescence into womanhood is the subject of a number of fairy tales, such as "Snow White," "Sleeping Beauty," "Beauty and the Beast," and "Cinderella," and he correctly notes a number of fairy-tale elements in this narrative, including an ancient château, a hunchback, and a foundling girl.[2] Yet in a way different from both fairy tales and Stendhal's previous novels, *Lamiel*, especially in its second version, is overtly a novel of education.

From the beginning, Lamiel is presented as a child of nature, as one who is most at ease with herself when romping through the woods or fields. Almost everyone, however, seems intent on teaching her – that is, leading her out of her wild state. Lamiel's adoptive father, Hautemare, is a teacher, and the Hautemares adopt Lamiel with the specific intention of educating her. They do teach her to read, but they are chiefly interested in seeing that she learn about sin and duty. As for the duchess, she undertakes to teach Lamiel conservative ideology and history, the aristocratic code of etiquette, and the literature produced by proper, noble ladies. Abbé Clément tutors Lamiel in history and English literature, while Fédor instructs her in vocabulary, literature, and geometry. Her foremost teacher, who occupies a prominent position only in the second version, is, however, a cynical, middle-aged doctor named Sansfin.

Sansfin is one of the more bizarre of Stendhal's characters. He is a hunchback ashamed of his hump and believes he can terrorize the local people into not noticing his deformity. As part of this strategy, he carries a loaded rifle at all times. It is even reported that he had once shot a man because he had made fun of his hump. The pain with which he bears his deformity has, moreover, instilled in him a sick jealousy of male beauty. Sansfin's condition is not meant to elicit our compassion, since the character is frequently treated from a comic point of view. His name, Sansfin, which translated literally means "without end," is itself humorous, and some scenes, such as the one describing his fall from his horse in front of a group of washerwomen, are clearly comic. Yet he is also a dangerous man, a villain who loves to manipulate others and for whom "the *word* crime had no meaning" (*L*, 42). He freely gives Lamiel medication that will make her condition worse, takes pleasure in tormenting the Duchess, and, with Lamiel's help, even stages a grotesque blood-spitting incident intended to further frighten her anxious benefactor.

This manipulative clown succeeds in making himself Lamiel's teacher in the ways of life. His "doctrine" is, in fact, quite simple: her parents are stupid and she must therefore never believe anything they say; crimes are to be marveled at (he reads to her daily the *Gazette des Tribunaux*, a newspaper that reports crimes currently being tried); and natural instincts should in all cases be followed. The world, he teaches Lamiel, is not divided into the rich and the poor but rather into dupes and rogues. Sansfin may be a despicable character in many ways, but some of his ideas echo to a degree Stendhal's own thinking. It is clear that Stendhal has no respect for religion such as that practiced by the Hautemares, that he had always admired great crimes and himself read the *Gazette des Tribunaux*, and that he subscribed to an ethos of pleasure. Stendhal is not Sansfin, to be sure (although he shares his consciousness of his ugliness), but he does not reject altogether his perverse moral code.

It is useful to consider Sansfin in relationship to Abbé Clément, whom Sansfin sees as his rival, for both play an important role in Lamiel's education. Clément shares one trait with Sansfin – namely, a good mind – but he differs from him radically on all other points. Indeed, the two of them provide a moral structure not unlike that found in the other novels. In *The Red and the Black*, *The Charter-house of Parma*, and, to a lesser extent, *Lucien Leuwen*, two women represent two different kinds of love that are also two possible ways to happiness. Here, two men, both of whom desire Lamiel, represent two competing approaches to life – cynicism and tenderness. Sansfin clearly wants to manipulate Lamiel and possibly seduce her. Clément loves her but forces himself to be harsh on her in order *not* to

seduce her. In his previous novels, Stendhal's male heroes all ultimately opt for the woman associated with tenderness, but Lamiel will
choose neither cynicism nor tenderness. Rather, she will hold out for
energy.

If Lamiel has had many teachers, it is also true that in many ways
she educates herself. It can be argued that she retains nothing at all
from the moral education she received from the Hautemares or even
Abbé Clément. Sansfin may inform her that her foster parents are
unintelligent, but she had already picked that up by overhearing a
remark by a neighbor. Her knowledge of physical love is gained by
paying for it, and she learns about life in general by being extremely
curious about everything. "Never was there a more inquisitive
being" (*L*, 107), writes the narrator. During her last days in Carville
she spent night and day reading, and we are told that in Paris she
spent most of her time with books. To be sure, she is strongly influenced by Sansfin's "moral" teaching, but that is in the second version, which covers only the first part of the story.

We do not know how extensive Sansfin's influence would have
been on her subsequent adventures in Rouen and Paris. It could be
argued that Sansfin's influence in the second version had fertile soil
on which to work, for already in the first version Lamiel emerges as
the only one of Stendhal's major characters to take pleasure in
hurting another person. After she has deceived Fédor, sent his
trunks on a coach to Cherbourg, robbed him, and surreptitiously left
for Paris, "she laughed and jumped with joy, imagining how troubled
the Duke would be when, arriving at the hotel, he would find neither
mistress, nor money, nor belongings" (*L*, 103). The obscurantism she
has experienced should not blind the reader to her capacity for
meanness.

The narrator tells us that, unlike other 16-year-old girls, Lamiel
"was not interested in love. What she liked above everything else was
an interesting conversation. A war story in which the hero braved
great dangers and accomplished difficult tasks caused her to day-
dream for three days, while she gave but passing attention to a love
story" (*L*, 53). She believes that she is insensitive to love and incapable of loving in any real way. In this respect she resembles Fabrice,
whose traits so differ from hers generally. Yet after concluding that
everyone is trying to deceive her about the nature of love, she is
taken with such a great curiosity on the subject that she loses her

virginity in a very deliberate manner by paying Jean Berville, a near-simpleton from her village, to deflower her. She finds only deception in the experience: "What! Is that all love is? . . . That famous love, it's only that?" (*L*, 67-68). In devaluing physical love, Stendhal is reaffirming an important theme of *On Love*. In narrating this episode, however, he is also boldly sketching a young woman who does not accept the passive role assigned to women in sexual relations. *She* decides when she will lose her virginity, and she does it "not in a moment of passion but out of simple curiosity" (Porter, 26).

Though desperately in love with Lamiel, Fédor is incapable of making love interesting for her. In Rouen Lamiel tells a hotel maid, "May God deliver me from lovers! I prefer my freedom above all else" (*L*, 99). She is initially attracted to Count D'Aubigné because, hearing that he has beaten a servant, she concludes that he has more energy than Fédor. His attractiveness increases when she learns of his plans to kill himself. Yet she quickly tires of him as well, and toward the end of the narrative she is still posing the same question: "Am I insensitive to love?" (*L*, 144). Stendhal's plans for the novel called for her to finally find love with a criminal named Valbaire in whom she finds "character." It is with him that "finally, she knows *love*" (*L*, 160).

Since Lamiel is the only principle female character in all Stendhal's work not to have inherited wealth, a number of critics have considered her a female Julien Sorel. As Gilbert Chaitin, among others, has pointed out, there are some striking resemblances between Lamiel's story and that of Julien Sorel. Both characters grow up in small provincial towns in lower-class families. During their adolescence, each enters the employ of the leading family of the town – Lamiel as a reader for the Duchess de Miossens, Julien as a tutor to the Rênal children. Each of them goes from the provincial town to the provincial capital and from there to Paris. They both acquire a "noble" name – Chevalier de la Vernaye for Julien, Madame de Saint-Serve for Lamiel. And *Lamiel* was to end with a crime, as did *The Red and the Black*.[3]

Like Julien, but also like other female characters such as Vanina Vanini, Mathilde, and Duchess Sanseverina, Lamiel is endowed with an exceptional character, a strong will, and tremendous energy. While she also resembles Julien in quickly seeing the weaknesses of others and in being quite ready to use deception as a means of self-protection, she is, on the other hand, clearly more daring than he is. He trembles at the thought of taking Madame de Rênal's hand, while she calmly pays someone to take her virginity. He agonizes over whether or not to accept Mathilde's invitation to come up to her room, while she boldly announces to Fédor that they will share an apartment in Rouen. Not only does she reverse the gender roles in courtship, but she does so without any of the internal debates that mark Stendhal's male heroes, especially Julien.

The problem of social class, so prominent in *The Red and the Black*, surfaces again in this novel, for without harboring Julien's bitter hatred of the upper classes, Lamiel is, like him, someone who climbs the social ladder. She begins as an orphan, moves up to the lower bourgeoisie through her adoption by the Hautemares and then to the aristocracy by sleeping with a duke and then a count, and then, finally, by marrying the duke. When Julien had arrived, he exulted that his novel was over. Lamiel does no such thing, for social ambition has never been one of her goals. Her marriage to the duke remains, by her decision, unconsummated so that she might remain faithful to her lover, Valbaire, who is from the lower classes. Yet we have the impression that her final choice of Valbaire is not a class option but a preference for energy.

The counterpoint to energy, boredom, a recurring theme throughout Stendhal's fiction, is clearly more striking in this novel than in any of Stendhal's others. Here boredom, with which Lamiel is afflicted from the age of 12, penetrates everything. Indeed, virtually all the novel's episodes can be related to a desire to flee boredom. The duchess's tedium accounts for Lamiel's success as a reader at the Château, just as the languor of château life is what leads to Lamiel's illness. Sansfin's influence on her is the result of her own weariness of the dull life around her. Lamiel is also bored with Fédor and then with D'Aubigné-Nerwinde. The answer to boredom is action and energy. From the beginning, Lamiel is referred to as restrained energy, being depicted at one point as a "chained gazelle" (*L*, 35). Although her movements, even the tempo of her gait, are severely restricted at the Château, as soon as she knows she is not observed she runs and jumps through the rooms. Her natural energies cannot be satisfied by the lethargic people around her. Writing from Civitavecchia to his friend Di Fiore, Stendhal expresses what surely are Lamiel's sentiments: "The only misfortune is to lead a boring life" (*Corr.*, 3:57).

Since Stendhal died before he could complete this novel, it is not possible to know what its ending would have been. Based on the outline Stendhal left, however, we have an idea of what he had been planning. In a three-page sketch, Stendhal has Lamiel fall in love with a notorious outlaw, Valbaire, a conclusion he had envisioned from the beginning. Early sketches made in 1839 call for Lamiel (then named Amiel) to fall in love with a thief and a murderer (then named Pintard). She was to be attracted by this outlaw's "true energy" (*L*, 9). Stendhal specifies that he is very ugly, so that Lamiel's love for him can be seen not as a physical attraction but as a yearning for energy. Unlike Sansfin, who is also ugly, this character makes no effort to hide his deformity and does not seem ashamed of it. Valbaire's naturalness, spontaneity, and energy finally unleash Lamiel's erotic drive. Now she can love, and it is Valbaire whom she loves.

The reader is prepared for Lamiel's foray into the underworld, since the narrator early on related Lamiel's fascination for stories of Cartouche and Mandrin, both notorious eighteenth-century outlaws whose courage and energy she admires. The reader also knows that Sansfin fed her a steady diet of readings from the *Gazette des Tribunaux*. In the sketch of the conclusion Lamiel agrees to a marriage of convenience with Fédor as a way of obtaining money to finance her criminal lover, Valbaire. After the latter is condemned to death and commits suicide, Lamiel sets fire to the courthouse in order to avenge his condemnation. The narrator concludes, "Some half-charred bones were found in the debris of the fire; they were Lamiel's" (*L*, 163). This act of arson against the symbol of order is her final message to a society that cannot countenance energy. Lamiel, whom everyone, it seems, had wanted to teach – who as an orphan might have seemed malleable – ultimately rejects attempts to civilize her. She ends her life as the most audacious of Stendhal's protagonists.

A Feminist Novel?

Some early currents of what might be called feminism were already evident in France in the 1830s. The Saint-Simonians, the Fourierists, and George Sand, among others, denounced the condition of women and called for reforms in female education and marriage laws. Stendhal, who had already made similar proposals in 1821 in *On Love*, had a longstanding interest in the condition of women. In numerous letters he had sought to educate his sister Pauline in a way that was then unconventional for women. On the intellectual level he had stressed the importance of her knowing empirical philosophy, mathematics, and history, while on the affective level he argued that happiness consists in being able to satisfy one's passions. In his fiction Stendhal consistently includes strong women characters. Simone de Beauvoir said of Stendhal (and of *Lamiel* in particular) that "he attempted a . . . rarer enterprise, one that I believe no novelist has before undertaken: he projected himself into a female character."[4]

Mina de Vanghel, in the story that bears her name, had affirmed a woman's right to make her own decisions. In *Lamiel*, particularly in the first version, the protagonist is a woman who affirms her right to choose and to act with complete freedom. It is worthy of note that when Lamiel announces to Fédor that they will live together in Rouen, she is not talking about a permanent commitment: "We'll live together, who knows? Ten days at least, until you begin to bore me" (*L*, 80). She tells him she does not love him and makes it clear that her freedom will always come first. In this sense, she is an oddity among nineteenth-century fictional women. Naomi Schor has argued that the nineteenth-century French heroine enjoys fewer freedoms than do her eighteenth-century counterparts, that the freedoms of Manon Lescaut and Marianne are not available to Eugénie Grandet and Madame Bovary.[5]

Since Lamiel is not readily understandable within the context of the nineteenth-century novel, many critics have either compared her to eighteenth-century heroines – not a surprising analogy since Stendhal's novelistic tastes, as Gita May has pointed out,[6] were clearly eighteenth-century – or have made of her a precursor to the twentieth-century woman. While it is true that in the second version of the first part of the novel Lamiel does fall under the influence of

Sansfin, it is not possible to say whether she would have freed herself from his influence in Stendhal's completed version. What seems
important is that Lamiel, in the first version that narrates her story
over a longer period of time, is a character who has an identity aside
from her relationship to men.

Concluding Remarks

While any study of Stendhal is bound to raise as many questions as it answers, some broad considerations emerge from a survey of his work. The first of these relates to Stendhal's consciousness of the genre. When novels are mentioned in Stendhal's fiction, they are inevitably referred to as frivolous writings whose pretensions he is quick to undermine. A case in point is Stendhal's now-famous comment after Julien has made love to Madame de Rênal: "One could have said, in the style of a novel, that there was nothing left to desire." Yet, paradoxically, in mocking the novels of his own time, Stendhal uses some of their more glaringly inept novelistic devices. There are incidents in Stendhal's novels that appear unworthy of a great novelist. The scene in which Octave writes to Armance in his own blood; the prediction based on an anagram in *The Red and the Black*; the staged birthing scene in *Lucien Leuwen*; and the blood-soaked sponge scene in *Lamiel* are but a few of the occasions that may disconcert a twentieth-century reader. Stendhal seems to delight in inserting in a serious novel, at a critical moment even, a novelistic device drawn from third-rate novels.

These procedures are, of course, part of the play of Stendhal's writing, for Stendhal wants to share with his readers his self-consciousness as a novelist, freely interrupting the narrative to address his "benevolent reader" and, on at least one occasion, to have a discussion with his publisher. We have noted Stendhal's playfulness as he intervenes in his text to criticize his own characters when in fact he admires their lyricism and sensitivity. This ludic propensity is also present in his affection for "para-stories," wherein the reader is invited to participate in the game of fictional creation: "If Julien had known . . . , he would have . . . " We sense Stendhal's pleasure in telling the story of two heroes – one the actual hero, the other a more astute hero. The play of creation thereby becomes a play with the reader as the writer teases the reader with announced elisions, puzzling titles, and glaringly misattributed epigraphs. Stendhal, a writer for whom seriousness and humor are always conjoined, invites his readers to participate in the play of the text and even in the production of meaning.

Stendhal's ties to the eighteenth century are not, then, only ideological but also narratological. As a nineteenth-century writer, he participates in the trend toward greater realistic representation, advocating an art that would portray all the forces acting on a society yet refusing a microrealism centered on descriptive detail. But, as Ann Jefferson has put it, Stendhal "sees representation as being determined more by the mental habits and the cultural expectations of the audience for whom it is constructed than by fidelity to the original events which it supposedly portrays" (Jefferson, 11). Realism implies selection, but the choice made by the writer necessarily occurs within the context of time, place, and audience. Stendhal's view of representation takes into account reader predisposition and reaction, and he sometimes tries to avert negative reactions through narratorial comments, admitting that what is about to be described or related will shock the reader. The famous passage assimilating the novel to the mirror in The Red and the Black is one such example. Stendhal wants to involve the reader in the act of representation. The ludic approach we have seen him use in his writing, however, is his reminder to his readers that literature does not truly represent reality, that all art contains illusion.

Furthermore, Stendhal is a writer with an acute sense of history, particularly of its rhythm and dynamics. Born under the ancien régime, he was a schoolboy during the Revolution, served in Napoleon's army and administration, lived in self-imposed exile during most of the Restoration, witnessed the revolution of 1830, and then served the July Monarchy as a diplomat. The confrontation between pre-Revolutionary and post-Revolutionary values that he constantly witnessed during his life became an important theme in his work. If his first hero, Octave, is destroyed, it is in part because he is caught between an ethical system of the past and a contemporary ethic, based on money, that he cannot accept. Octave knows perfectly well – and on this point he is one of the most lucid aristocrats in Stendhal's fiction – that the nobility is finished as a class. The most pitiful aristocrats in Stendhal's work are the Duchess de Miossens in Lamiel and the Marquis de Pontlevé in Lucien Leuwen, both of whom refuse to acknowledge the movement of history and take refuge in the illusion that the past can exist in the present.

Stendhal nonetheless distinguishes himself from other writers of his time in not accepting the thesis of historical progress. His was a cyclical view of human development, whereby great societies appear and disappear at various periods. The heroic eras of the past were more of an inspiration to him than was the dream of an ideal society to come. He recognized that governments of the future, however different they might be from the despotisms of yesteryear, would also be, in their own way, forces of oppression. He understood – consider in this instance *Lucien Leuwen* – that a government that controls the means of communication and has at its disposal large sums of money would easily trounce its opposition. Since his death, some have tried to pin a political label on Stendhal, to make of him an author of the Right or the Left. While his political leanings were left of center, he remained cynical about politics, and his work is an indictment of all government of whatever stripe.

What is perhaps the most striking from a political point of view is the complexity of alliances and associations that can be found in his fiction. Two of his young right-wing nobles, Octave de Malivert and Fédor de Miossens, attended the Polytechnical School, then recognized as a progressive institution. In *The Red and the Black* a fierce liberal reformer, Monsieur Appert; an elderly Jansenist, Abbé Chélan; and a reactionary nobleman, Marquis de la Mole, are friends and allies. In the same novel Altamira, an Italian revolutionary, is a friend of Jansenists and a guest in royalist drawing rooms, while a plebeian with strong Bonapartist sentiments – namely, Julien – serves as an agent in an ultraroyalist conspiracy. In *The Charterhouse of Parma* Mosca, who fought in Spain for Napoleon, is the prime minister of a reactionary regime. There are explanations for these associations and alliances, but the fact that they exist is proof that Stendhal shuns political reductionism.

What interests Stendhal are not so much political institutions as such but rather, and especially, the reverberations of political institutions on individuals. All of Stendhal's heroes are adolescents on the verge of becoming adults, and, in this sense, his novels are novels of education or initiation. The two first heroes, Octave and Julien, define themselves before being. Neither Octave nor Julien lives his own life; rather, both try to live according to a preconceived model – Octave, a model of duty and Cornelian honor; Julien, a model of Napoleonic ambition. They do so, however, with this difference: Octave cannot surpass his own mythology. A prisoner of a conception he has created of himself, he ends his life through suicide. Julien, when he is in prison, succeeds not only in surpassing his own mythology but also in seeing through it and understanding its falsity.

The two heroes who follow, Lucien Leuwen and Fabrice del Dongo, do not, however, define themselves before being but are characters in search of self-definition. Lucien's anguished statement, "In truth, I don't know what I am," and Fabrice's question, "What am I?," echoing Stendhal's own self-questioning in *The Life of Henry Brulard*, are clear indications among many others that neither has a preconceived idea of his own essence. Lucien, however, is related to the previous heroes by the fact that he does not accept himself. If he does not know what he is, he believes himself nevertheless obliged to act in such a way as not to displease others. Fortunately, in the last pages of the novel, he does attain the insight that pleasing himself is what matters most. Fabrice, on the other hand, is the first of Stendhal's major characters to accept himself. "I forgive myself for my fear," he says in one moment of self-acceptance. For Lamiel, the question does not even come up. The distance traveled since Octave's tortured self-questioning can be accounted for by the discovery of a sense of self and the formulation of a new relationship to the other.

As would be the case a century later for Sartre, the fear of the judgment of others is, for Stendhal's characters, the source of suffering. They are acutely aware of the judgmental eye of others, so much so that one of their constant desires is to see without being seen. Hell, as Sartre put it, is other people. The evolution of the Stendhalian hero, which begins with Julien's consciousness at the end of *The Red and the Black*, eventually leads in *The Charterhouse of Parma* to a situation in which the characters want to see and be seen. Fabrice is in love and, since this time love is not filtered through a Cornelian or Napoleonic mythology or through the image of a father, the gaze of others is not feared but sought. At the summit of his work Stendhal redefines hell as no longer being able to love. Love is what destroys the fear of others. The eye of the other, which destroys because it judges, is not to be feared by the one who can surpass his own ego and thereby arrive at true passionate love.

Stendhal's work is the evocation of the primacy of passionate love. It is not by chance that Julien and Fabrice find salvation in prison. Love and passion can be attained but not sustained in the politicized life of their times. Love, the great dream, can be experienced to the full only in exceptional circumstances (in prison, while awaiting execution, or in a mythical Italy) – or in the novels of Stendhal.

Notes and References

Chapter One

1. See Richard N. Coe, Translator's Preface to *The Lives of Haydn, Mozart, and Metastasio* (London: Calder & Boyars, 1972), xxii.

2. For a discussion of these qualities as they apply to Stendhal's work generally, see Jean-Pierre Richard, *Littérature et sensation* (Paris: Editions du Seuil, 1954).

Chapter Two

1. In an 1828 article on Duras's *Olivier* Stendhal stated that "it will never be published. The nature of the subject had led the author into dangerous territory. . . . M. de Stendhal has nevertheless undertaken to face this danger, and a second edition of *Armance* is currently in press" (*Courrier anglais*, vol. 3, ed. H. Martineau [Paris: Le Divan, 1935], 365).

2. Henri Bussière, "Henri Beyle (M. de Stendhal)," *Revue des Deux-Mondes*, 15 January 1843, 291.

3. *Causeries du lundi*, vol. 9 (Paris: Garnier, n.d.), 328.

4. "Obstacle Race," in *Music at Night and Other Essays* (London: Chatto & Windus, 1949), 157.

5. Chateaubriand, *Atala. René*, ed. Pierre Reboul (Paris: Garnier-Flammarion, 1964), 176; hereafter cited in text.

6. See C. W. Thompson, "Les Clefs d'*Armance* et l'ambivalence du génie romantique du Nord," *Stendhal-Club* 25 (1982-83): 520-47.

7. André Gide, Preface to *Armance* (Geneva: Cercle du Bibliophile, n.d.), xviii; H.-F. Imbert, *Les Métamorphoses de la liberté ou Stendhal devant la Restauration et le Risorgimento* (Paris: Corti, 1967), 372; the latter hereafter cited in text.

8. Shoshana Felman, *La "Folie" dans l'oeuvre romanesque de Stendhal* (Paris: Corti, 1971), 169; hereafter cited in text.

9. See his *S/Z* (Paris: Seuil, 1970), 22-23, 171.

10. F. W. J. Hemmings, *Stendhal: A Study of His Novels* (Oxford: Oxford University Press, 1964), 73; hereafter cited in text.

11. G. Mouillaud, "Stendhal et le monde irréel: A propos de l'impuissance dans *Armance*," *Modern Language Notes* 83 (1968): 535; Felman, 174.

12. André Gide, *La Porte étroite* (Paris: Mercure de France, 1959), 145.

13. André Stegmann, *L'Héroïsme cornélien: Genèse et signification*, vol. 2 (Paris: Colin, 1968), 279.

14. See George M. Rosa, "Byronism and 'Babilanisme' in *Armance*," *Modern Language Review* 77 (1982): 801.

15. Eric Gans, "Le Secret d'Octave: Secret de Stendhal, secret du roman," *Revue des sciences humaine* 187 (1975): 87.

16. On the similarities in personality between Armance and Octave, see Charles O'Keefe, "A Function of Narrative Uncertainty in Stendhal's *Armance*," *French Review* 50 (1977): 582.

17. André Malraux, *La Voie royale* (Paris: Editions Lidis, 1961), 14.

18. Victor Brombert, *Stendhal: Fiction and the Themes of Freedom* (New York: Random House, 1968), 56; hereafter cited in text.

Chapter Three

1. Robert Alter, *A Lion for Love* (New York: Basic Books, 1979), 189.

2. Gérald Rannaud, "Un aspect du 'réalisme' chez Stendhal: Ecriture romanesque et perception économique," in *Stendhal/Balzac: Réalisme et cinéma*, ed. V. Del Litto (Paris: Editions du CNRS, 1978), 154.

3. Michel Arrous, "Le Séminaire dans *Le Rouge et le Noir* (Limites du réel et fonction romanesque)," *Stendhal-Club* 20 (1977): 68.

4. Erich Auerbach, *Mimesis: The Representation of Reality in Western Literature* (New York: Doubleday, 1957), 403; hereafter cited in the text.

5. Paul Jourda, *Stendhal raconté par ceux qui l'ont vu* (Paris: Stock, 1931), 143.

6. *Journal des Débats*, 26 December 1830.

7. For a full discussion of this issue, see Serge Bokobza, *Contribution à la titrologie romanesque: Variations sur le titre "Le Rouge et le Noir"* (Geneva: Droz, 1986).

8. On this particular issue see chap. 6 of Bokobza, "Et: La binarité et la contradiction," 119-28.

9. Ann Jefferson, *Reading Realism in Stendhal* (Cambridge: Cambridge University Press, 1988), 108; hereafter cited in text.

10. Jean-Jacques Hamm, "*Le Rouge et le Noir* d'un lecteur d'épigraphes," *Stendhal-Club* 20 (1977): 20.

11. Stirling Haig, *Stendhal: The Red and the Black* (Cambridge: Cambridge University Press, 1989), 31.

12. Albert Sonnenfeldt, "Ruminations on Stendhal's Epigraphs," in *Pre-text/Text/Context: Essays on Nineteenth-Century French Literature*, ed. Robert M. Mitchell (Columbus: Ohio State University Press, 1980), 108; hereafter cited in text.

13. For a discussion of this probability, see Grahame C. Jones, "Réel, Saint-Réal: Une épigraphe du *Rouge* et le réalisme stendhalien," *Stendhal-Club* 25 (1983): 235-43.

14. Armand Hoog, "Le 'rôle' de Julien," *Stendhal-Club* 20 (1978): 131-42; hereafter cited in text.

15. See his *Stendhal et la voie oblique* (Paris: Presses Universitaires de France, 1954).

16. Benjamin Bart, "Hypercreativity in Stendhal and Balzac," *Nineteenth-Century French Studies* 3 (1975): 18-39.

17. James T. Day, *Stendhal's Paper Mirror: Patterns of Self-Consciousness in His Novels* (New York: Peter Lang, 1987), 14.

18. Peter Brooks, "The Novel and the Guillotine; or, Fathers and Sons in *Le Rouge et le Noir*," *PMLA* 97 (1982): 352.

19. For a broader discussion of this issue, see Lane Gormley, " 'Mon roman est fini': Fabricateurs de romans et fiction intratextuelle dans *Le Rouge et le Noir*," *Stendhal-Club* 21 (1979): 129-38.

20. Geneviève Mouillaud, *"Le Rouge et le Noir" de Stendhal: Le Roman impossible* (Paris: Larousse, 1973), 36.

21. See, for example, Martin Turnell, *"Le Rouge et le Noir,"* in *Stendhal: A Collection of Critical Essays*, ed. Victor Brombert (Englewood Cliffs, N.J.: Prentice-Hall, 1962), 21.

22. Elizabeth Brody Tennenbaum, *The Problematic of Self: Approaches to Identity in Stendhal, D. H. Lawrence, and Malraux* (Cambridge: Harvard University Press, 1977), 46.

23. John Mitchell, *Stendhal: Le Rouge et le Noir* (London: Edward Arnold, 1973), 50.

Chapter Four

1. Jean Prévost, *La Création chez Stendhal* (Paris: Mercure de France, 1951), 293; hereafter cited in text.

2. Michel Crouzet, *Quatre Etudes sur "Lucien Leuwen"* (Paris: SEDES, 1985), 71.

3. Christof Weiand, "En marge de *Lucien Leuwen*: *L'Orange de Malte*: Titre ou énigme," *Stendhal-Club* 96 (1982): 450-58.

4. Martine Reid, "Peut-être, ou *Lucien Leuwen* inachevé," in *Le Plus méconnu des romans de Stendhal: "Lucien Leuwen,"* ed. Philippe Berthier et al. (Paris: SEDES, 1973), 72.

5. David Place, "Stendhal's Rhetoric of Love in *Lucien Leuwen*," *Modern Language Review* 74 (1979): 48.

Chapter Five

1. Jean-Jacques Rousseau, *Les Confessions*, ed. J. Voisine (Paris: Garnier, 1964), 3; hereafter cited in text.

2. Philippe Lejeune, "Stendhal et les problèmes de l'autobiographie," in *Stendhal et les problèmes de l'autobiographie*, ed. V. Del Litto (Grenoble: Presses Universitaires de Grenoble, 1976), 22.

3. Richard N. Coe, "Stendhal, Rousseau, and the Search for the Self," *Australian Journal of French Studies* 16 (1979): 28; hereafter cited in text.

4. V. Del Litto, Preface to *Oeuvres intimes*, vol. 1 (Paris: Gallimard, 1981), xxxii.

5. Mireiella Melara, "Stendhal's Autobiographical Narrative: (Re)collecting Ruins, Fragments, and Pieces of Fresco," *Romantic Review* 79 (1988): 319.

6. See, on this subject, Martine Reid, "Représentation d'Henri Beyle," *Poétique* 65 (1986): 34-35.

7. Henri Martineau, *L'Oeuvre de Stendhal* (Paris: Albin Michel, 1966), 449.

8. "I wrote my *Confessions* . . . from memory; my memory frequently failed me or furnished me but imperfect recollections, and I filled in the gaps with details that I imagined as a supplement to my recollections" (*Oeuvres complètes*, vol. 1, ed. Bernard Gagnebin and Marcel Raymond [Paris: Gallimard, 1959], 1035).

9. Psychoanalytical critics have argued that some of these gaps have as their purpose to elide aspects of his life that are too painful to allow to surface. See, as an example of this approach, Carol A. Mossman's suggestive essay "Death and Transfiguration in the *Vie de Henry Brulard*," *Studies in Romanticism* 26 (1987): 527-47.

10. On the subject of the engravings, see Carol Mossman, "Iconographie brulardienne: Les Figures d'une écriture," *Stendhal-Club* 28 (1986): 339-53.

11. Dennis Porter, "Stendhal and the Impossiblity of Autobiography," *French Studies* 32 (1978): 164; hereafter cited in text.

12. Béatrice Didier, *Stendhal autobiographe* (Paris: Presses Universitaires de France, 1983), 234; hereafter cited in text.

13. Jean Starobinski, *L'Oeil vivant* (Paris: Gallimard, 1961), 194.

14. Michel Crouzet, *La Vie de Henry Brulard ou l'enfance de la révolte* (Paris: Corti, 1982), 19-20.

Chapter Six

1. Anna Maria Scaiola, " 'Ce qu'il y a de plus terrible et plus doux' : Béatrice Cenci," in *Stendhal, Roma, l'Italia,* ed. M. Colesanti et al. (Rome: Edizioni di Storia e Letteratura, 1985), 466.

2. Hans Boll-Johansen, "Une théorie de la nouvelle et son application aux *Chroniques italiennes* de Stendhal," *Revue de littérature comparée* 50 (1976): 427; hereafter cited in text.

3. For a fuller discussion of this dimension, see Franc Schuerewegen, "Le Détective défaillant ou l'instance du policier dans les *Chroniques italiennes,*" *Orbis Litterarum* 39 (1984): 213-29.

4. See on this point Claudine Vercollier, "La Parole assassine: Le Dialogue dans *L'Abbesse de Castro,*" *Stendhal-Club* 29 (1987): 282-90.

5. Philippe Berthier, "Topo-energétique de *L'Abbesse de Castro,*" *Stendhal-Club* 28 (1986): 137.

Chapter Seven

1. On this subject see Emile J. Talbot, "Stendhal, the Artist, and Society," *Studies in Romanticism* 13 (1974): 213-23.

2. See on this subject Eugene Goodheart, "Aristocrats and Jacobins: 'The Happy Few' in *The Charterhouse of Parma,*" *Yale Review* 65 (1976): 370-91.

3. For a full discussion of these archetypal markings, see Gilbert Durand, *Le Décor mythique de "La Chartreuse de Parme"* (Paris: Corti, 1961).

4. Emile Talbot, *La Critique stendhalienne de Balzac à Bourget* (York: French Literature Publications, 1979), 64.

5. Robert M. Adams, *Stendhal: Notes on a Novelist* (New York: Minerva Press, 1968), 84.

6. Stephen Gilman, *The Tower as Emblem* (Frankfurt am Main: Klostermann, 1967), 37-46.

7. C. W. Thompson, "Répétition, jeu et destin dans *La Chartreuse de Parme,*" in *Stendhal/Balzac: Réalisme et cinéma,* 190. See also his *Le Jeu de l'ordre et de la liberté dans "La Chartreuse de Parme"* (Aran: Editions du Grand-Chêne, 1982) for a fuller discussion of this important topic.

8. See Herbert Morris, *The Masked Citadel: The Significance of the Title of Stendhal's "La Chartreuse de Parme"* (Berkeley: University of California Press, 1968).

9. Victor Brombert, *La Prison romantique: Essai sur l'imaginaire* (Paris: Corti, 1975), 69.

10. Philippe Berthier, "Stendhal n'a jamais appris à écrire ou l'incipit," in *La Chartreuse de Parme revisitée,* ed. Philippe Berthier (Grenoble: Université Stendhal-Grenoble III, 1990), 31.

Chapter Eight

1. Leanne Wierenga, "Stendhal's *Lamiel*: A Re-evaluation," Ph.D. diss., University of Illinois, 1975, 38-40.

2. Dennis Porter, "*Lamiel*: The Wild Child and the Ugly Men," *Novel* 12 (1978): 24; hereafter cited in text. See the entire article for a more extended discussion of this aspect of the novel.

3. Gilbert D. Chaitin, *The Unhappy Few: A Psychological Study of the Novels of Stendhal* (Bloomington: Indiana University Press, 1972), 174.

4. Simone de Beauvoir, *The Second Sex*, trans. and ed. H. M. Parshley (New York: Knopf, 1953), 247.

5. Naomi Schor, *Breaking the Chain: Women, Theory, and French Realist Fiction* (New York: Columbia University Press, 1985), 135-46.

6. Gita May, "Le Féminisme de Stendhal et *Lamiel*," *Stendhal-Club* 20 (1978): 192.

Selected Bibliography

PRIMARY WORKS

French Texts

The most complete and authoritative edition of Stendhal's works is the 50-volume *Oeuvres complètes*, edited by V. Del Litto and E. Abravanel (Geneva: Cercle du Bibliophile, 1967-74). First editions are as follows:

Armance. Paris: Urbain Canel, 1827.

Le Rouge et le Noir. 2 vols. Paris: Levavasseur, 1831.

La Chartreuse de Parme. 2 vols. Paris: Ambroise Dupont, 1839.

Lucien Leuwen. Paris: E. Dentu, 1894. The first part of the novel was published under the title *Le Chasseur vert* in the volume *Nouvelles inédites*. Paris: Michel Lévy, 1855.

Lamiel. Paris: Librairie moderne, 1889.

La Vie de Henry Brulard. Paris: Charpentier, 1890.

English Translations

The Short Novels of Stendhal. Translated by C. K. Scott-Moncrief. New York: Liveright, 1946. Contains "Armance," "The Abbess of Castro," "Vittoria Accoramboni," "The Cenci," "The Duchess of Palliano," and "Vanina Vanini."

Red and Black. Translated by Robert M. Adams. New York: Norton, 1969.

Lucien Leuwen. Translated by H. L. R. Edwards. London: Penguin, 1991.

The Charterhouse of Parma. Translated by C. K. Scott-Moncrief. New York: Signet, 1962.

The Pink and the Green. Translated by Richard Howard. New York: New Directions, 1988.

Lamiel. Translated by T. W. Earp. New York: New Directions, 1952.

The Life of Henry Brulard. Translated by Jean Stewart and B. C. J. G. Knight. Chicago: University of Chicago Press, 1986.

Memoirs of an Egotist. Edited and translated by David Ellis. London: Chatto & Windus, 1975.

The Private Diaries of Stendhal. Edited and translated by Robert Sage. New York: Doubleday, 1954.

Rome, Naples, and Florence. Translated by Richard N. Coe. New York: G. Braziller, 1960.

Memoirs of a Tourist. Translated by Allan Saeger. Evanston, Ill.: Northwestern University Press, 1962.

Travels in the South of France. Translated by Elisabeth Abbott. New York: Orion Press, 1970.

A Life of Napoleon. New York: Howard Fartig, 1977.

Life of Rossini. Edited and translated by Richard N. Coe. London: Calder & Boyers, 1975.

Love. Translated by Gilbert and Suzanne Sale. London: Penguin, 1975.

SECONDARY WORKS

Alter, Robert. *A Lion for Love: A Critical Biography of Stendhal.* New York: Basic Books, 1979. A highly readable biography that combines insight into the man with perceptive criticism of his work.

Berthier, Philippe. *Stendhal et ses peintres italiens.* Geneva: Droz, 1977. The best discussion available on Stendhal's important relationship to Italian painting. Includes perceptive commentary on the presence of Guido Reni's and Il Guercino's styles in Stendhal's writings and an enlightened discussion of the Correggian atmosphere of *The Charterhouse of Parma.*

Bloom, Harold, ed. *Stendhal's "The Red and the Black."* New York: Chelsea House, 1988. A collection of essays by René Girard, Harry Levin, D. A. Miller, Peter Brooks, Ann Jefferson, Margaret Mauldon, and Carol A. Mossman. All these essays have been published previously, and all are first rate.

Boll-Johansen, Hans. *Stendhal et le roman: Essai sur la structure du roman stendhalien.* Aran: Editions du Grand-Chêne, 1979. An intelligent and lucid discussion of the narrative structure of Stendhal's novels. Contains original insights on the role of women, the function of secondary characters, novelistic temporality, point of view, and sequential structure.

Brombert, Victor. *Stendhal: Fiction and the Themes of Freedom.* New York: Random House, 1968. Brief and incisive discussion of the themes of freedom as they interact with social, political, psychological, and ethical concerns.

Coe, Richard N. "Stendhal, Rousseau, and the Search for the Self." *Australian Journal of French Studies* 16 (1979): 27-47. Stendhal emerges from this first-rate comparative study as highly aware of the problems and pitfalls of autobiography and as the creator of a new species of the genre.

Crouzet, Michel. *Stendhal ou Monsieur Moi-Même*. Paris: Flammarion, 1990. The most comprehensive biography to date, written by a leading Stendhal scholar.

Day, James T. *Stendhal's Paper Mirror: Patterns of Self-Consciousness in His Novels*. New York: Peter Lang, 1987. Argues that while Stendhal's novels do reflect contemporary reality, they mostly reflect themselves and their own fictional narration. Contains useful studies of some of the strategies Stendhal uses to call attention to the problematics of narration.

Didier, Béatrice. *Stendhal autobiographe*. Paris: Presses Universitaires de France, 1983. Thorough discussion of all of Stendhal's autobiographical writings, including the journal, with important insights into the representation of space, memory, and the discipline required of an author who writes about himself.

Felman, Shoshana. *La "Folie" dans l'oeuvre romanesque de Stendhal*. Paris: Corti, 1971. A solid study of Stendhal's use of the theme of madness, including important analyses of *Armance* and *The Charterhouse of Parma*.

Finch, Alison. *Stendhal: "La Chartreuse de Parme."* London: Edward Arnold, 1984. An excellent introduction to the novel.

Haig, Stirling. *Stendhal: "The Red and the Black."* Cambridge: Cambridge University Press, 1989. An excellent introduction to Stendhal's best-known novel.

Hamm, Jean-Jacques. *Le Texte stendhalien: Achèvement et inachèvement*. Sherbrooke: Naaman, 1986. A probing analysis of the relationship between completeness and incompleteness in Stendhal, leading to the conclusion that incompleteness is a fundamental characteristic of his work.

Jefferson, Ann. *Reading Realism in Stendhal*. Cambridge: Cambridge University Press, 1988. A successful attempt to shed new light on the subject of Stendhal and realism by positing at the outset that mimesis as practiced by Stendhal takes a different form from those that provide objective records of exterior reality.

Pearson, Roger. *Stendhal's Violin: A Novelist and His Reader*. Oxford: Clarendon Press, 1988. A significant look at Stendhal the novelist and his relationship to his reader. Proposing that Stendhal's novelistic project is to provide for multiple readers, Pearson concentrates his analysis on Stendhal's four major novels.

Porter, Dennis. "*Lamiel*: The Wild Child and the Ugly Men." *Novel* 12 (1978): 21-32. Cogently argues that Lamiel follows the schema of the fairy tale while making a decisive break with that schema in the ending, which is not only unhappy but also violent.

Reid, Martine. "Correspondences: Stendhal en toutes lettres." *Yale French Studies* 71 (1986): 149-68. Brilliant commentary on the function of letter writing in Stendhal's total writing project, with some consideration of the function of letters in his fiction.

Thompson, C. W. *Le Jeu de l'ordre et de la liberté dans "La Chartreuse de Parme."* Aran: Editions du Grand-Chêne, 1982. An excellent discussion of *The Charterhouse of Parma* by a critic who is alert to the differences and discontinuities among Stendhal's novels. Special attention is paid to the relationship between order and freedom, and to to the importance of play in bringing about an equilibrium among freedom, rules, and change.

Tillet, Margaret. *Stendhal: The Background to the Novels.* London: Oxford University Press, 1971. Concentrating on Stendhal's concept of *"l'âme généreuse,"* Tillet provides good coverage of most of Stendhal's nonfiction.

Index

The Author

Emile J. Talbot, a native of Maine, received his graduate degrees from Brown University and is currently professor of French and comparative literature and head of the Department of French at the University of Illinois at Urbana-Champaign. His primary research areas are nineteenth-century French literature and Canadian literature. His previous work on Stendhal includes *La Critique stendhalienne de Balzac à Zola* (1979) and *Stendhal and Romantic Esthetics* (1985). He has been a fellow of the National Endowment for the Humanities, the Center for Advanced Study of the University of Illinois, and the Camargo Foundation. He is a member of the editorial boards of *Nineteenth-Century French Studies*, *Québec Studies*, and *La Revue francophone*.

The Editor

David O'Connell is professor of foreign languages and chair of the Department of Foreign Languages at Georgia State University. He received his Ph.D. from Princeton University in 1966, where he was a National Woodrow Wilson Fellow, the Bergen Fellow in Romance Languages, and a National Woodrow Wilson Dissertation Fellow. He is the author of *The Teachings of Saint Louis: A Critical Text* (1972), *Les Propos de Saint Louis* (1974), *Louis-Ferdinand Céline* (1976), *The Instructions of Saint Louis: A Critical Text* (1979), and *Michel de Saint Pierre: A Catholic Novelist at the Crossroads* (1990). He is the editor of *Catholic Writers in France since 1945* (1983) and has served as review editor (1977-79) and managing editor (1987-90) of the *French Review*.